D0796341

THE
NATIONAL
AIR
AND SPACE
MUSEUM

Acknowledgments

My participation in this volume grew out of an idle dinner conversation in Chicago with Ian Ballantine who, by casually mentioning old airplanes, inadvertently touched upon a childhood fascination with all things that flew that has continued in me up to the present. Our talk inevitably turned from there to one of my favorite places, the Smithsonian Institution, for I had been a steady visitor to the old Air Museum ever since it had opened in a Quonset off to one side of the "Castle." Moreover, my interest was clearly shared by more than twenty million people who had visited the new National Air and Space Museum in its first two years. When Ian mentioned that Harry N. Abrams, Inc., had an agreement with the Smithsonian Institution for publishing an authorized book on their new Museum, I immediately volunteered to write the text. Ever since that evening I have been assisted, educated, instructed, amused, and indulged by highly specialized men and women of the National Air and Space Museum staff whose knowledge and expertise are but imperfectly reflected by my text.

I could not have undertaken this work without the assistance and encouragement of Ian Ballantine and Harry N. Abrams, Inc.'s President Andrew Stewart and Digby Diehl, his editor-in-chief; nor would the work have progressed so pleasurably and smoothly without the extraordinarily able and professional Abrams' staff—in particular editor Edith Pavese and designer Nai Chang; but the book was made possible only by the complete and eager cooperation we all received from the staff of the National Air and Space Museum. In behalf of us all I would like to single out certain individuals whose unstinting giving of their time and expertise are owed recognition in print.

Michael Collins, Under Secretary of the Smithsonian Institution, and Melvin B. Zisfein, Deputy Director of NASM, lent their authority and approval to this project and made it possible for me to work from the Museum galleries' concept scripts. This pattern of management support continues under the new Director, Dr. Noel W. Hinners. Executive Officer Walter J. Boyne personally guided me through the Silver Hill Museum complex and the *Enola Gay*'s bomb bay, and subsequently guided the text through its rockier channels. Public Information Officer Lynne Murphy, her successor Rita Bobowski, and Staff Assistant Louise Hull provided invaluable contacts and administrative assistance.

It is said that a museum is only as good as its collection; but a collection is only as good as its curators. Paul Garber, NASM's Historian Emeritus, was responsible for many of the Museum's earliest acquisitions. Charles H. Gibbs-Smith, NASM's first Lindbergh Professor of Aerospace History, was extremely helpful with information on the Wrights. In the Aeronautics section, however, our gratitude is owed Assistant Director of Aeronautics Donald S. Lopez; Curator of Aircraft Louis S. Casey; Curator of Propulsion Robert B. Meyer; and Curators Robert C. Mikesh and Edmund T. Wooldridge. A very special thanks to Assistant Curator Claudia M. Oakes whose uncluttered writing and thinking, encouragement, knowledge, and humor made things far easier than they would otherwise have been. Thanks, too, to Museum Technician Jay P. Spenser and Museum Specialist Supervisor Elmont J. Thomas of the Aeronautics section.

Frederick C. Durant III, Assistant Director of Astronautics, was embarrassingly patient in answering my questions about spacecraft principles and generous in sharing his knowledge and appreciation of space pioneer Robert H. Goddard. If the space sections of this text appear at all learned they reflect the invaluable assistance and expertise of Walter H. Flint and Tom D. Crouch, Curators of Astronautics, and Gregory P. Kennedy and Walter J. Dillon, Assistant Curators.

Curator of Art James Dean was gracious enough to permit some of his art treasures to be sprinkled throughout this book despite the fact that the Art Gallery displays the collection more as a unified whole. And we thank, too, Bill Good and Mary Henderson of the Art Department for so generously giving their time.

I would like to acknowledge a special "writer's debt" to the Museum's Reference Librarian Dominick A. Pisano who tracked down some wonderful stories and leads, and Karl P. Suthard, a Technical Information Specialist in the Library. And for his help at the Silver Hill Museum, our gratitude to Edward Chalkley, that Museum complex's Assistant Chief.

Hernan Otano, Chief of the Audiovisual Unit, Richard Wakefield, A/V Supervisor, Electronic Technicians John Hartman and Daniel Philips, Exhibit Section's Chief of the Production Unit Frank Nelms, Exhibit Specialist Sylvandous Anderson, Painter Daniel Fletcher and Carpenter Milan Tomasevich all generously shared their materials, equipment, experience, and time.

Howard Wolko, Assistant Director of the Science and Technology section, and Curators Richard Hallion and Paul Hanle helped me feel almost comfortable in writing about what had previously been incomprehensible. I am grateful, too, to Robert W. Wolfe, a geologist with the Center for Earth and Planetary Studies, for his assistance and Von Del Chamberlain, Chief of the Presentations Division, and Patricia Woodside for their help on the Albert Einstein Spacearium section.

Joseph Davisson, NASM's Building Manager, Claude Russell, Assistant Building Manager, Supervisor Mary Whittaker, and Artifacts Crewman Larry Johnson helped make the inaccessible accessible. Captain Preston Herald III, Captain of the Museum's Protection Division, and his staff saw that we were able to freely wander about.

And finally, I would like to acknowledge my genuine debt to a great many writers who have so generously permitted me to quote from their articles and books.

C.D.B. Bryan
Guilford, Conn.

THE NATIONAL AIR AND SPACE MUSEUM

Volume Two
SPACE

Text by **C.D.B. BRYAN**

Art Direction & Design by **DAVID LARKIN**

Photographed by MICHAEL FREEMAN, ROBERT GOLDEN, and DENNIS ROLFE

PEACOCK PRESS/BANTAM BOOKS
Toronto   New York   London   Sydney

to my great-great uncle

CAPT. JOHN RANDOLPH BRYAN, C.S.A.

who, as aide-de-camp to General J. B. Magruder, made
three balloon ascensions for the Army of the Peninsula,
the last of which, on May 5, 1862, became an
inadvertent free flight because a young soldier became
entangled in the guide-rope connecting the balloon to
the ground. When in order to prevent the young
soldier from being dragged into the winch the tether
rope was cut, the "balloon bounded two miles into the
air. First it drifted over the Union lines, then was
blown back toward the Confederate lines near
Yorktown. The Confederates, seeing it coming from
that direction, promptly opened fire. Finally it
skimmed the surface of the York River, its guide-rope
splashing in the water, and landed in an orchard. On
this trip the balloon made a half-moon circuit of about
fifteen miles, about four miles of which was over the
York River."*

*The Photographic History of the Civil War, Francis Trevelyan Miller,
editor-in-chief, New York: The Review of Reviews Co., 1911

THE NATIONAL AIR AND SPACE MUSEUM
VOLUME TWO • SPACE
A Bantam Book / published by arrangement with
Harry N. Abrams Inc.

PRINTING HISTORY
Abrams edition published September 1979
A Selection of Book-of-the-Month Club, Spring 1980

Bantam edition / October 1982

Project Editor: Edith M. Pavese
Assistant Editor: Margaret Donovan
Design Copyright © 1979, 1982 by
David Larkin, Becontree Press

Library of Congress Cataloging in Publication Data

Bryan, Courtlandt Dixon Barnes.
    National Air and Space Museum. Volume Two, Space.
    Includes index.
    1. National Air and Space Museum.   I. Title.
TL506.U6W373   629.1'074'0153   79-1432

ISBN 0-553-01385-8

Published simultaneously in the United States and Canada

Bantam Books are published by Bantam Books, Inc. Its trademark,
consisting of the words "Bantam Books" and the portrayal
of a rooster, is Registered in U.S. Patent and Trademark Office
and in other countries. Marca Registrada.
Bantam Books, Inc., 666 Fifth Avenue, New York, New York 10103.

PRINTED IN THE UNITED STATES OF AMERICA

0 9 8 7 6 5 4 3 2 1

Grateful acknowledgment is made for permission to quote from
the following works:

Oral Histories from the Oral History Research Office, Columbia
University, (Lt. Macready) Copyright 1974, (Lt. Leslie P. Arnold)
Copyright 1979, and (Frank Coffyn) Copyright 1979 by the
Trustees of Columbia University and The City of New York.

The Washington Post, June 27, 1976. Copyright © 1976 The
Washington Post.

MAN AND SPACE, a volume of Life Science Library, by Arthur
C. Clarke and the Editors of Time-Life Books, Copyright 1964
and 1969 Time, Inc.

WE SEVEN, BY THE ASTRONAUTS THEMSELVES by M. Scott
Carpenter, Copyright 1962 by Simon & Schuster, Inc., by
permission of Simon & Schuster, a Division of Gulf & Western
Corporation.

CARRYING THE FIRE by Michael Collins, Copyright © 1974 by
Michael Collins, by permission of Farrar, Straus & Giroux, Inc.

FIRST ON THE MOON by Neil Armstrong, Michael Collins,
Edwin E. Aldrin, Jr., with Gene Farmer and Dora Jane
Hamblin, Copyright © 1970 by Little Brown & Co., by
permission of the publisher.

The London Economist, July 26, 1969, Copyright 1969 by The
Economist Newspaper Ltd., London.

A HOUSE IN SPACE by Henry S. F. Cooper, Jr., Copyright 1976
by Henry S.F. Cooper, Jr. Reprinted by permission of Holt,
Rinehart and Winston, Publishers.

The National Geographic Magazine, Vol. 160, No. 4, October
1981. "Our Phenomenal First Flight" by John Young and
Robert Crippen.

Contents

Rowland Emett's S.S. Pussiewillow II, *a whimsical moving sculpture of a futuristic spacecraft, delights visitors to the Museums' Flight and the Arts' gallery.*

The Smithsonian Institution, ever since its founding in 1848, had evidenced its interest in aerospace development. Joseph Henry, the first Secretary of the Institution, successfully persuaded President Abraham Lincoln to support balloonist Thaddeus S. C. Lowe's utilization of captive balloons by the Northern Army for military observation during the Civil War. The Institution's collection of aeronautical objects began in 1876 when a group of kites was acquired from the Chinese Imperial Commission. Samuel P. Langley, the third Secretary of the Institution (and a trained astrophysicist who established the Smithsonian Astrophysical Observatory) was smitten by the allure of flight in his late fifties and became one of aviation's most controversial and unlucky aerial pioneers. He did nevertheless manage to produce in 1896 the first American heavier-than-air powered flying machine capable of making a free flight of any significant length. His machine, Langley's Aerodrome #5, containing a one hp steam engine, was launched from a houseboat on the Potomac River, and flew about 3,000 feet at a speed of almost 25 mph before landing gently in the river. The model hangs near the wall of the Milestones of Flight gallery. When Langley attempted to build a man-carrying machine based on an enlargement of his successful model's design, he failed.

The fourth Secretary of the Institution, Charles D. Wolcott, and Smithsonian Regents Alexander Graham Bell and Ernest W. Roberts, realizing the need to place American aviation on a sound scientific footing, began actively petitioning Congress for an aeronautical research and policy center in 1912. As a result of their efforts, the National Advisory Committee for Aeronautics (the forerunner of NASA) was created in 1915. The following year the Smithsonian began its long association with Robert H. Goddard, the "father" of modern rocketry. For the next twenty-nine years the Smithsonian not only published Goddard's major articles but assisted in providing funds for his research.

In July 1929 one of Goddard's tests with his fledgling rockets at his Aunt Effie's farm outside of Worcester, Mass., created such an earsplitting din that police, ambulances and reporters rushed out to the farm thinking a disaster had occurred. One newspaper headlined MOON ROCKET MISSES TARGET BY 238,799½ MILES and the police forbade Goddard to carry out any more tests. None of Goddard's rockets had reached an altitude of more than 90 feet and yet, that November when Charles A. Lindbergh visited Goddard at the farm, Goddard said he thought he would be able to build a rocket capable of carrying scientific instruments to altitudes approaching one hundred miles and that it would even be possible to build a multistage rocket capable of reaching the moon. "It might cost a million dollars," Goddard added, implying the expense of building such a rocket was beyond consideration. And yet forty years later, on July 16, 1969, Lindbergh was present at Cape Kennedy as a guest of the astronauts to watch the launch of Apollo 11 to the moon at an expenditure of twenty-five *billion* dollars. Four days later, on July 20, 1969, while astronaut Michael Collins circled in lonely orbit in the Apollo 11 command module *Columbia*, astronauts Neil Armstrong and Edward Aldrin dropped down to the surface in the lunar module and became the first men to walk on the moon.

Goddard's early rockets, Langley's Aerodrome #5, Lindbergh's tiny, silver *Spirit of St. Louis*, Armstrong, Aldrin and Collins'

When on July 6, 1976, the National Air and Space Museum officially opened its doors to the first of the approximately ten million visitors it has received each year, it seems appropriate that the *Museum's first director* in the new building should have been Michael Collins. He might have been speaking for all those visionaries whose dreams the Museum so wondrously celebrates when, on September 16, 1969, Collins addressing a joint session of Congress had said:

MR. SPEAKER, MR. PRESIDENT, MEMBERS OF CONGRESS AND DISTINGUISHED GUESTS:
Many years before there was a space program, my father had a favorite quotation: "He who would bring back the wealth of the Indies, must take the wealth of the Indies with him." This we have done. We have taken to the moon the wealth of this nation, the vision of its political leaders, the intelligence of its scientists, the dedication of its engineers, the careful craftsmanship of its workers, and the enthusiastic support of its people.

We have brought back rocks, and I think it's a fair trade. For just as the Rosetta Stone revealed the language of ancient Egypt, so may these rocks unlock the mystery of the origin of the moon, and indeed even of our earth and solar system.

During the flight of Apollo 11, in the constant sunlight between the earth and the moon, it was necessary for us to control the temperature of our spacecraft by a slow rotation, not unlike that of a chicken on a barbeque spit. As we turned, the earth and the moon alternately appeared at our windows. We had our choice. We could look toward the moon, toward Mars, toward our future in space, toward the New Indies, or we could look back toward the earth, our home, with the problems spawned over more than a millennium of human occupancy.

We looked both ways. We saw both, and I think that is what our nation must do. We can ignore neither the wealth of the Indies nor the realities of the immediate needs of our cities, our citizens, our civics.

We cannot launch our planetary probes from a springboard of poverty, discrimination, or unrest; but neither can we wait until each and every terrestrial problem has been solved. Such logic two hundred years ago would have prevented expansion westward past the Appalachian Mountains, for assuredly, the Eastern seaboard was beset by problems of great urgency then, as it is today.

Man has always gone where he has been able to go. It's that simple. He will continue pushing back his frontier, no matter how far it may carry him from his homeland.

Someday in the not-too-distant future when I listen to an earthling step out onto the surface of Mars or some other planet, as I heard Neil step out onto the surface of the moon, I hope to hear him say: "I come from the United States of America."

This book is an attempt to capture some of the National Air and Space Museum experience. Whenever possible we have supplemented the text with personal reminiscences, eyewitness accounts, or written records of some of the men who designed or flew the spacecraft, these wondrous machines on exhibit which helped push back our frontiers as we continue on our voyage to the New Indies of space.
Apollo 11 command module *Columbia* rest within feet of each other within the National Air and Space Museum's Milestones of Flight gallery. Time, space, adventure, heroism, dreams overlap in that huge, treasure-filled room. One of the first letters Michael Collins received following Apollo 11's triumphant return was from the man whose lonely, daring, exhausting and dangerous non-stop 3,600-mile flight from New York across the cold, stormy, unforgiving Atlantic to Paris had so thrilled the world just over two score years before. "What a fantastic experience it must have been," Lindbergh wrote Collins, "alone, looking down on another celestial body, like a god of space! There is a quality of aloneness that those who have not experienced it cannot know—to be alone and then to return to one's fellow man once more. You have experienced an aloneness unknown to man before."

Milestones of Flight

Stand in the center of the huge Milestones of Flight gallery and look up at that frail canvas and wood biplane skimming overhead. It is the Wright Flyer, and at 10:35 on the morning of Thursday, December 17, 1903, it clattered down its two-by-four inch board launching track and lifted itself into the air over the level sands near Kill Devil Hill, North Carolina, and for twelve engine-popping, chain-rattling seconds of uneven darting flight that machine carried Orville Wright about 100 feet through the air until it struck the ground. It was the first time in history that a man-carrying machine had lifted itself into the air under its own power, had sailed forward without slowing, and had landed on ground as high as that from which it had taken off.

Beneath and to the left of the Wright Flyer stands an odd-looking array of pipes and tubes that looks part-factory steam whistle, part-incompleted scaffolding. It is a model of Robert H. Goddard's and the *world's* first successful liquid propelled rocket. On March 16, 1926, it rose 41 feet in the air, attained a speed of about 60 mph and arced 184 feet downrange before hitting the ground.

The duration of Goddard's rocket's first flight, like that of the Wright Flyer, could be measured only in seconds, but its significance has reverberated through the years with ever increasing importance. The Wright Brothers gave us the means to fly through the air; Goddard gave us the means to fly into space.

Fifty years and about as many feet separate Goddard's first liquid-fuel rocket from the newest addition to the Milestones of Flight gallery: a Viking Lander. The Viking Landers were the first spacecraft to conduct extended scientific studies on the surface of another planet. On July 20, 1976, ten months and 400-million miles after it had been launched and exactly seven years after man had first walked on the moon, earthbound computers transmitted one word to instruct the Viking Lander to separate from its orbiting spacecraft and begin its descent to the surface of Mars. The word: KVUGNG. Almost twenty minutes later the Lander dropped from its orbit hundreds of miles above the Red Planet and streaked downward through the late afternoon Martian sky. At an altitude of about 25 miles the thin atmosphere began to slow the capsule, at about four miles up a huge parachute was deployed and the Lander slowed even more. A little more than one mile over the surface of Mars three rocket engines fired to retard the capsule's fall. Soon the parachute was cut loose and the Viking Lander settled on the Martian soil with no more impact than a skydiver landing upon his target and the rocket engines shut down. Instantly the computer signalled earth that the Lander was on Mars, that it was intact, and that it was beginning work. Moments later, Earth's TV screens began to fill with the historic first photograph ever seen of the surface of Mars. The picture showed Viking 1's footpad resting firmly on a surface made of fine soil and scattered rock. Even after being transmitted more than 200 million miles, the photograph was so clear tiny pebbles appeared in sharp detail. The Lander next sent a stunning 300-degree panoramic photograph of the rolling, rocky sector of the Martian basin called Chryse Planitia upon which it had landed.

On September 3, 1976, a second Viking spacecraft successfully landed on the more rolling plains of Utopia and it too immediately began transmitting back scientific data. Both Viking orbiters continued to conduct photographic surveys of the planet's surface for the next two years.

The Viking 2 Lander was shut down on April 11, 1980; the Viking 1 Lander continues to send meteorological and engineering data and photographs to earth essentially on a weekly basis. The Lander on display is the Proof Test Capsule used for performance tests and simulations before and during the actual mission. The full color photograph displayed with the Viking was taken by Viking 2 and it shows Mars' characteristic red soil and pinkish sky. On July 25, 1976, in an appreciation of the success of the Viking project, the *New York Times* in an editorial wrote:

> Time as well as space have in a sense been conjoined. The instrument that has performed this miracle is that inhuman little robot, sending out its signals, a mere creature of another miracle whose power is even more spectacular than that of all the Vikings and Mariners put together—the miracle of the human mind.

It is the miracle of the human mind that, more than anything else, the Museum's Milestones of Flight gallery celebrates, for as one looks about the gallery at those other air and spacecraft which marked such milestones in the history of flight, one sees the "milestones" themselves becoming progressively more mysterious and complex, more difficult to appreciate, to measure than a flight from point-to-point. As each new plateau was crossed by the individual or individuals in each machine, the flight technology demanded less and less of the individual and more and more the effort of groups, of teams of scientist-engineers, test-pilot mechanics, astronaut-scholars, physicists and theoreticians. The machines, themselves, seem to resemble airplanes less and less and devices more and more— scientific tools designed for specific purposes, to increase understanding and knowledge. The machines' designs begin to reflect their purpose and even in cases such as the deep space probes, mechanical manifestations of pure thought itself. When the visitor, for example, looks at that stubby-

winged, bright orange and white bullet-shaped aircraft hanging high up near the gallery's west wall, he is seeing a needle-nosed Bell X-1, *Glamorous Glennis,* designed to pierce the sound barrier.

During the later stages of World War II, pilots of advanced fighter aircraft experienced strange and alarming behavior on the part of their machines when in a high-speed dive they approached the speed of sound. Their planes buffeted, wrenched about, controls sometimes reversed or became ineffective, increased drag set in; in some cases, the wings tore off, the plane broke apart and crashed. Because of these experiences there developed the idea of a sonic wall, a "sound barrier" of some kind through which no aircraft could pass unscathed. In 1944 the National Advisory Committee for Aeronautics (NACA) and the U.S. Army Air Forces initiated a cooperative program to explore this wall. For this purpose the Bell X-1 was designed and cautiously tested, its rocket-engine permitted to fire just long enough to creep the little plane's speed increment by increment up to the speed of sound. And then on October 14, 1947, Captain Charles E. "Chuck" Yeager flew the experimental *Glamorous Glennis* (named after Yeager's wife) 700 mph at 43,000 feet and thereby became the first man to fly beyond the speed of sound. Describing the flight later, Yeager reported:

> With the stabilizer setting at 2° the speed was allowed to increase to approximately .98 to .99 Mach number where elevator and rudder effectiveness were regained and the airplane seemed to smooth out to normal flying characteristics. This development lent added confidence and the airplane was allowed to continue to accelerate until an indication of 1.02 on the cockpit Mach meter was obtained. At this indication the meter momentarily stopped and then jumped to 1.06 and this hesitation was assumed to be caused by the effect of shock waves on the static source. At this time the power units were cut and the airplane allowed to decelerate back to the subsonic flight condition. When decelerating through approximately .98 Mach number a

*The Bell X-1, the first plane to fly beyond
the speed of sound (1947).*

This "brute of a machine" was designed to bridge the gap between manned flight in the atmosphere and manned flight in space; the rocket-powered X-15 was the first to fly four, five, and six times the speed of sound.

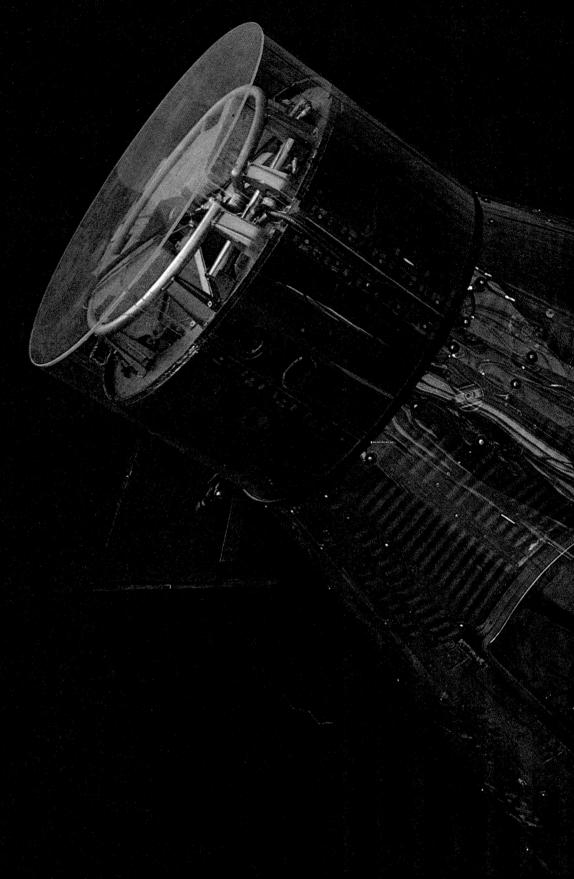

Gemini 4 EVA: A mannequin in the
Milestones of Flight gallery depicts Edward
H. White II becoming the first American to
"walk in space."

single sharp impulse was experienced which can best be described by comparing it to a sharp turbulence bump.

—*Supersonic Flight: The Story of the Bell X-1 and Douglas D-558*, by Richard Hallion

The fact that nothing "spectacular" had happened belies the significance of that flight. When on August 26, 1950, General Hoyt Vandenberg as Air Force Chief of Staff presented the X-1 to Dr. Alexander Wetmore, then Secretary of the Smithsonian Institution, he stated that the aircraft "marked the end of the first great period of the air age, and the beginning of the second. In a few moments the subsonic period became history, and the supersonic period was born."

Diagonally across from the Bell X-1 is the North American X-15, that big, black, ugly brute of a machine to which the supersonic period gave birth. In 1963 this rocket-propelled research aircraft flew higher (354,000 feet), and in 1967, faster (4,534 mph) than any other airplane in history. An X-15 became the first aircraft to fly Mach 4, Mach 5, and Mach 6—four, five, and six times the speed of sound. It was designed to bridge the gap between manned flight within the atmosphere and manned flight beyond the atmosphere in space and to study hypersonic aerodynamics, control systems, winged reentry from space, and aerodynamic heating. Because of its high-speed capability, the X-15 had to withstand aerodynamic temperatures of 1,200° F.; the aircraft was therefore manufactured using a special high-strength, heat-resistant nickel alloy. The X-15 was airlaunched from a special modified Boeing B-52; the rocket-powered plane required conventional aerodynamic control surfaces to operate within the atmosphere and special "thruster" reaction control rockets located in the nose and wings to permit the pilot control of the X-15 when flying in the thin atmospheric fringe of space. The wedge-shaped tail surfaces were needed for control at high speeds. Because the X-15's tail surface arrangement was a cruciform in shape, the lower half of the ventral fin was designed to be jettisonable prior to landing so that the rocket craft could land on a conventional two-wheel nose-landing gear and two tail-mounted landing skids. Three X-15 aircraft were built; they completed a total of 199 research flights which resulted in at least 700 technical documents, an amount equivalent to the output produced by a typical 4,000-man federal research center in the course of two years.

Beneath the Bell X-1 rests the Mercury spacecraft *Friendship 7*. On the morning of February 20, 1962, while 135 million Americans watched on their television sets or listened in on their radios, Marine Lt. Col. John Glenn was rocketed into space in that spacecraft from Cape Canaveral (briefly renamed Cape Kennedy), Florida, and became the first American to orbit the earth.

Glenn circled our planet three times at an altitude which varied between 101 and 162 miles and at a speed of 17,500 mph. The flight took 4 hours and 55 minutes and demonstrated to U.S. scientists that the human body could safely function in the weightlessness of space and that the U.S. spacecraft was safe for manned missions. Below are excerpts from the first radio voice messages exchanged between Astronaut Glenn and Mercury Control at Cape Canaveral on the morning that the United States truly entered the manned space exploration race.

CC stands for Cape Canaveral, P represents the pilot, John Glenn. The numerals show the flight time in hours, minutes, and seconds following the countdown and lift off.

	CC	[Cape Canaveral] . . . 5, 4, 3, 2, 1, lift off!
00 00 03	P	[Pilot] Roger. The clock is operating. We're under way.
00 00 07	CC	Hear [you] loud and clear.

Bill, 508 +08
Pid
039
KM

TL 506, UG W3

Friendship 7. *the Mercury spacecraft in which John Glenn, on February 20, 1962, became the first American to orbit the earth.*

00 00 08	P	Roger. We're programming in roll okay.
00 00 13	P	Little bumpy along about here.
00 00 48	P	Have some vibration coming up here now.
00 00 52	CC	Roger. Reading you loud and clear.
00 00 55	P	Roger. Coming into high Q [vibration] a little bit; and a contrail went by the window, or something there.
00 01 00	C	Roger.
00 01 12	P	We're smoothing out some now, getting out of the vibration area.
00 01 16	CC	Roger. You're through max. Q. Your flight path is...
00 01 19	P	Roger. Feels good, through max. Q and smoothing out real fine.
00 01 31	P	Sky looking very dark outside.
00 02 07	CC	Roger. Reading you loud and clear. Flight path looked good. Pitch, 25. Stand by...
00 02 12	P	Roger. The [escape] tower fired; could not see the tower go, I saw the smoke go by the window.
00 02 36	P	There, the tower went by right then. Have the tower in sight way out. Could see the tower go. Jettison tower is green.
00 04 08	P	Friendship Seven. Fuel 103−101 [percent], oxygen 78−100, amps 25, cabin pressure holding steady at 5.8.
00 04 20	CC	Roger. Reading you loud and clear. Seven, Cape is Go; we're standing by for you.
00 04 25	P	Roger. Cape is Go and I am Go. Capsule is in good shape...All systems are Go.
00 05 12	P	Roger. Zero G, and I feel fine. Capsule is turning around.
00 05 18	P	Oh, that view is tremendous!
00 05 21	CC	Roger. Turnaround has started.
00 05 23	P	Roger. The capsule is turning around and I can see the booster during turnaround just a couple of hundred yards behind me. It was beautiful.
00 05 30	CC	Roger. Seven. You have a Go, at least seven orbits.
00 05 35	P	Roger. Understand Go for at least seven orbits.

The vocabulary: *Max Q, Zero G, escape towers, boosters, separation;* the phrases: *we're programming in roll, all systems are go;* the *count-downs* and *lift-offs*...how swiftly we have become accustomed to the language of the space age!

The Mercury flights were the first of three steps that formed the United States' response to President John F. Kennedy's challenge a year before Glenn's flight, that "This nation should commit itself to achieving the goal, before this decade is out, of landing a man on the moon and returning him safely to Earth." The second step, the Gemini project, is represented by the Gemini 4 spacecraft located below the X-15. It was in this 7,000-pound spacecraft launched into orbit on June 3, 1965, that astronaut Edward H. White opened the right-hand hatch and "floated" out into space connected to the Gemini 4's life support and communications systems by only a gold-covered "umbilical cord." His "walk" proved that astronauts could work effectively outside their spacecraft, for example, on the lunar surface. White maneuvered by using a hand-held thruster. Other Gemini flights proved that man could stay up long enough to get to the Moon and back. This led to the Apollo program.

Directly beneath the X-15 stand two diminutive progenitors of the towering Atlas, Titan, and Saturn rockets that lifted our astronauts; they are a full-scale model of Dr. Robert H. Goddard's first liquid-propellant rocket built in 1926, and Dr. Goddard's actual final rocket built in 1941. These rockets, representing the beginning and the end of Dr. Goddard's efforts to develop high-altitude liquid-propellant rockets, mark the

Edward H. White floating in space connected to Gemini 4's life-support system only by his gold "umbilical cord."

first major breakthrough on our way to the exploration of space.

The first of Dr. Goddard's rockets to be successfully flown is the one on the metal tubular stand. It was launched from a farm in Massachusetts on March 16, 1926, and reached an altitude of 41 feet, powered by liquid oxygen and gasoline. The flight lasted but 2½ seconds, and the rocket's average speed was approximately 60 mph; but, like the first tentative flights of the Wrights' Flyer, the 1926 rocket marked the dawn of a new age. During the flight a portion of the rocket's nozzle was burned away and other parts were damaged when the rocket impacted into the ground 184 feet from its launch site; but the rocket was repaired, its pieces reassembled, and the rocket flown again on April 3, 1926.

The larger rocket was one of the last and most advanced liquid-propellant rockets tested by Dr. Goddard between 1939 and 1941. The rocket on display made several flights and was rebuilt several times. The significance of this rocket, however, is that it incorporated most of the basic principles and elements such as fuel pumps and cooling systems used later in all long-range rockets and space boosters.

High up near the ceiling is a small silver ball with "antennae" extending from it; it is a model of Sputnik 1, the first man-made object to be placed in orbit around the earth. Sputnik (meaning traveling companion) was launched, on October 4, 1957, atop a 96-foot-tall Soviet military rocket whose 1,124,440 pounds of thrust boosted the 184-pound satellite into orbit. For 22 days Sputnik 1 transmitted internal and external temperature information and provided important orbital data concerning atmospheric and electronic densities at high altitudes. This model, on loan from the U.S.S.R. Academy of Sciences, commemorates certainly one of the most dramatic milestones. The actual satellite, of course, burned up on reentry into the earth's atmosphere on January 4, 1958.

On November 3, 1957, the Soviets further stunned the world by placing Sputnik 2 into orbit. This artificial satellite weighed 1,121 pounds and carried Laika, a dog, into orbit. On December 6, 1957, Vanguard Test Vehicle 3, carrying the first American earth satellite, a small grapefruit-sized device, exploded on its launch pad and the United States' prestige reached a new low. In France café waiters the next morning approached American tourists and sardonically asked if they would like a "grapefruit" for breakfast.

Finally, on January 31, 1958, a four-stage Jupiter-C rocket designed, built and launched by the Army Ballistic Missile Agency team headed by Wernher von Braun, successfully placed Explorer 1, the first American satellite, in orbit. The back-up spacecraft hangs near the Sputnik 1 model above the balcony overlooking the Milestones gallery. Explorer 1 measured three phenomena: cosmic ray and radiation levels (thus providing data which, when combined with data obtained from Explorer 3, later that year, led to the discovery of the Van Allen belts, the belts of radiation surrounding the earth named after James Van Allen of the University of Iowa, one of the team who prepared the satellite's instrumentation), the temperature within the vehicle (essential knowledge in the design of future manned spacecraft), and the frequency of collision with micro-meteorites. The American Explorer 1 satellite weighed 30.8 pounds including its fourth stage.

Sputnik 1 and Explorer 1 marked the opening stages of man's space adventure. By January, 1975, 1,734 payloads had been fired into space; 1,007 had been destroyed reentering the earth's atmosphere, but 684 were still in orbit and 43 were orbiting the sun or rushing out into deep space. Among them is Mariner 2, a replica of which hangs in the Milestones gallery. On December 14, 1962, Mariner 2 was launched, making a 109-day trip that took it 36 million miles from earth to within 21,600 miles of Venus, thus completing the first successful mission to another planet. In the Milestones of Flight gallery is also a replica of the Pioneer 10

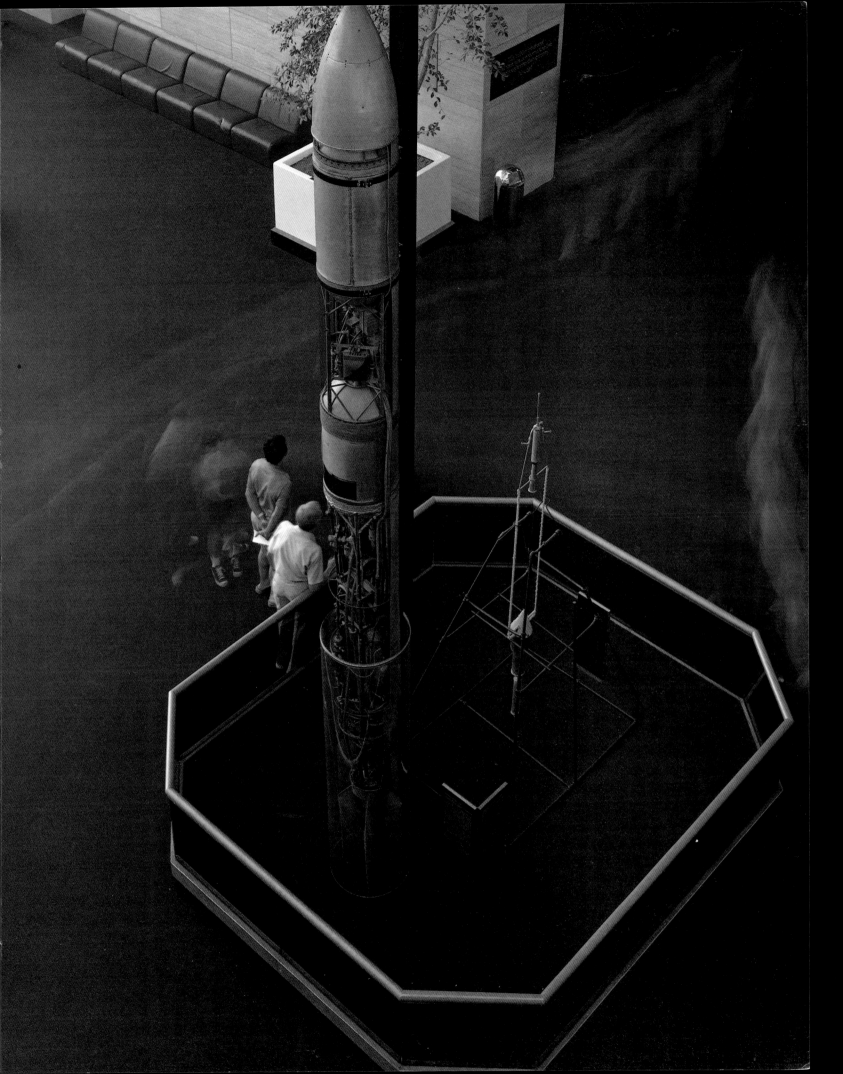

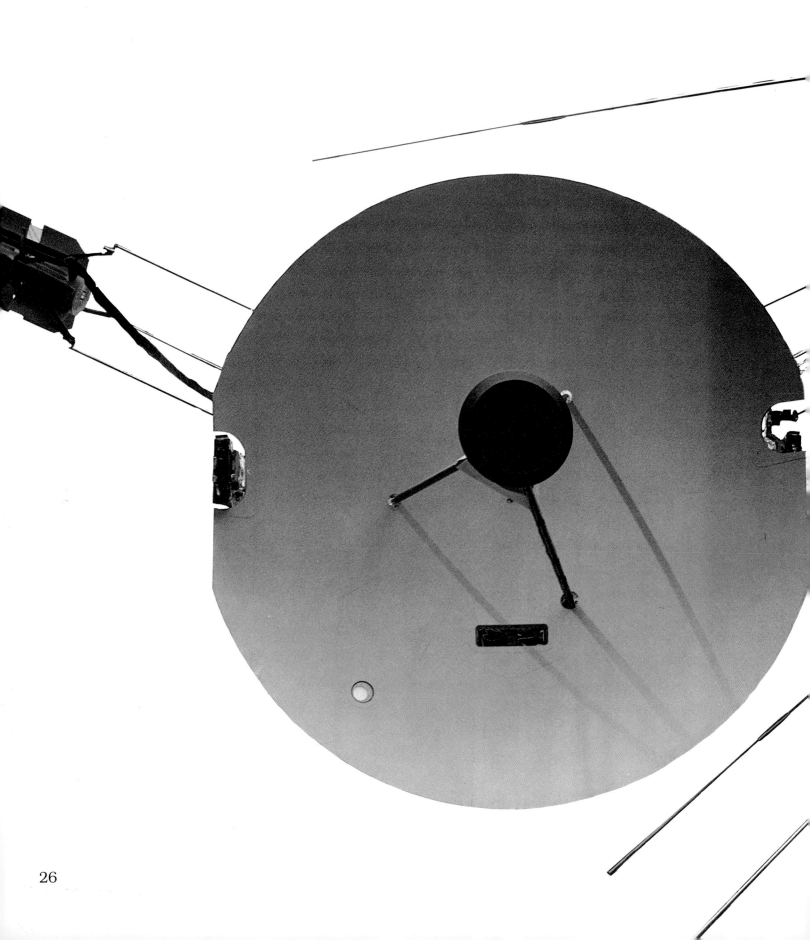

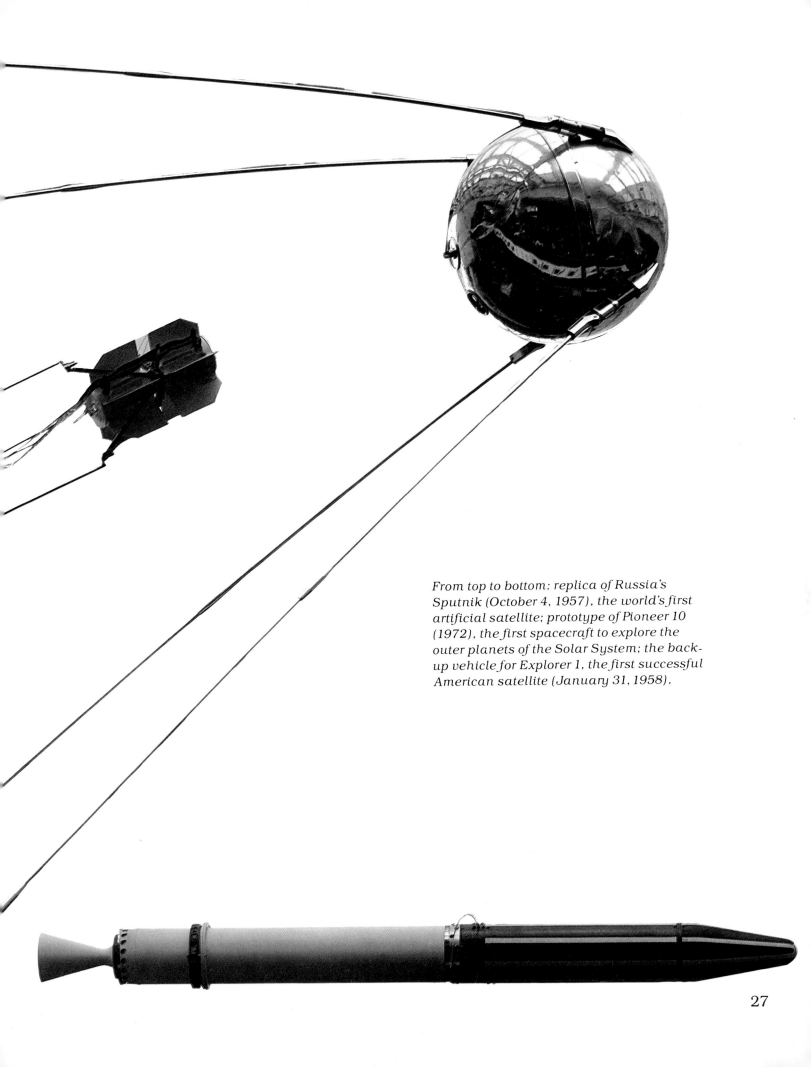

From top to bottom: replica of Russia's Sputnik (October 4, 1957), the world's first artificial satellite; prototype of Pioneer 10 (1972), the first spacecraft to explore the outer planets of the Solar System; the back-up vehicle for Explorer 1, the first successful American satellite (January 31, 1958).

(hanging between Sputnik 1 and Explorer 1, which was launched on March 3, 1972, and was the first spacecraft to explore the outer planets of the Solar System. On December 3, 1973, the Pioneer 10 spacecraft passed within 82,000 miles of Jupiter and transmitted scientific information and photographs of the planet's surface 515 million miles back to earth. In 1990, Pioneer 10 will pass the farthest point of Pluto's orbit and continue on out through the Solar System. It carries a plaque designed to inform any intelligent extra-terrestrial life about the spacecraft and where it came from. This spacecraft was launched with the highest speed ever achieved for a man-made object: 31,122 mph. It seems somehow especially appropriate that the Pioneer 10 spacecraft which was launched unmanned to explore the farthest reaches of our Solar System should hang so close to the Langley Aerodrome #5, which was launched unmanned also, on May 6, 1896, and was the first American heavier-than-air flying machine to make a free flight of any significant length. It flew about 3,000 feet at 25 mph from a houseboat on the Potomac River for about a minute and a half in several broad circles before landing gently on the river.

Two identical Viking spacecraft were launched from the Kennedy Space Center: Viking 1, launched August 20, 1975 and Viking 2 on September 9, 1975. The general objectives of the Viking mission were: "To increase significantly man's knowledge of the planet Mars through orbital observations by the orbiter as well as by direct measurements made by the lander during Martian atmospheric entry, descent and landing . . . . Particular emphasis was placed on obtaining biological, chemical and environmental data relevant to the existence of life on the planet at the present time, at some time in the past, or the possibility of life existing at a future date. Orbiter observations consisted of radio-science, imaging, thermal and water vapor measurements used to assist landing-site selection and the study of the dynamic and physical characteristics of Mars and its atmosphere. Lander direct measurements consisted of radio-science, atmospheric structure and composition, landing-site imaging, atmospheric pressure, temperature and wind velocity, identification of the elemental composition of the surface material, the search for evidence of living organisms and organic materials, and determination of seismological characteristics of the planet. The Viking scientific return was further expanded by the capability of simultaneous Martian observations from orbit and the surface."

Successful soft landings on the surface of Mars were made on July 20, 1976 by Viking 1 and on September 3, 1976 by the Viking 2 Lander. The Viking 2 orbiter was shut down when its attitude control gases, depleted by a leak, ran out on July 24, 1978. The Viking 2 Lander was shut down on April 11, 1980 due to battery failure and the inability of its own radio transmitters to broadcast directly to the Earth tracking stations. The Viking 1 orbiter ran out of steering fuel on August 7, 1980. The Viking 1 Lander continues to send meteorological data, engineering data and photographs to Earth essentially on a weekly basis.

Orange-red materials cover most of the surface of Mars, apparently forming a thin layer over darker rocks exposed in some patches. Scientists think the reddish material might be limonite or hydrated ferric oxide, which forms on Earth in the presence of water and an oxidizing atmosphere. The color of Mars' sky, described as "pink to a kind of creamy orange" is probably the result of scattering and reflection of light from the reddish dust suspended in the thin Martian atmosphere.

This Viking Lander was used before and during the Viking missions as a testing model. It could just as easily have been one of the two that are now on the surface of Mars.

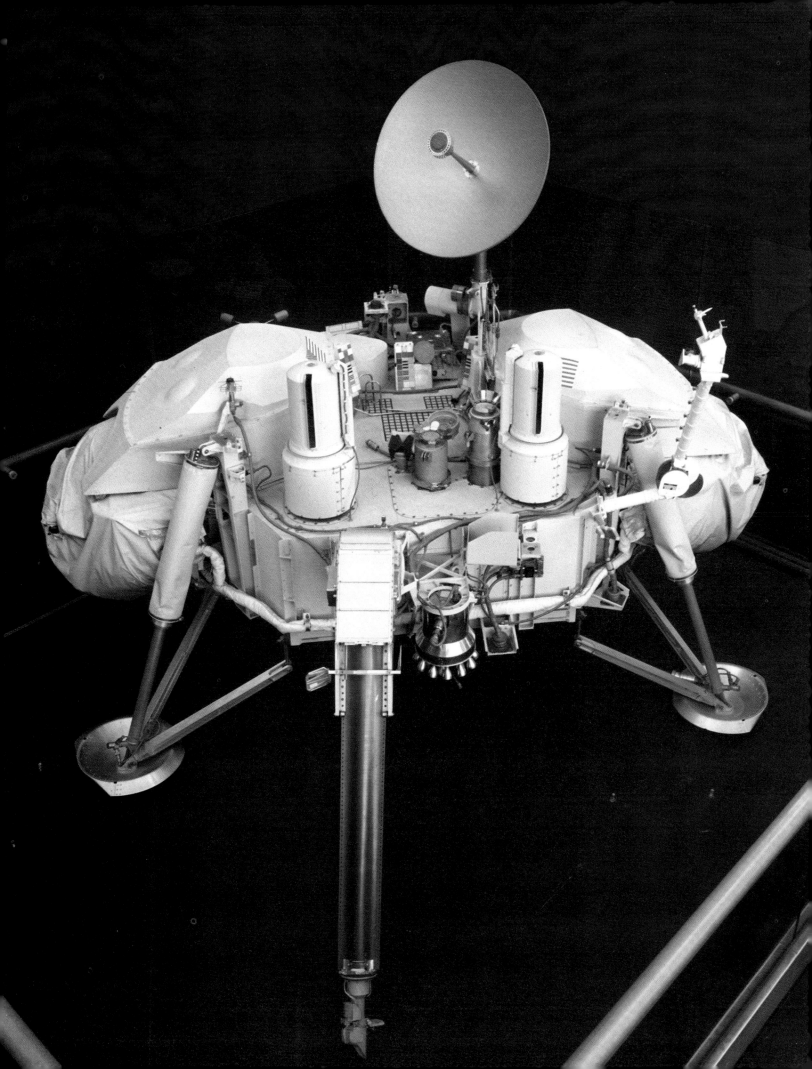

As we complete our circle of the Milestones of Flight gallery, our eyes quite naturally return to the 1903 Wright Flyer and the large, conical spacecraft beneath it. The spacecraft is the Apollo 11 command module in which astronauts Neil Armstrong, Edwin Aldrin, and Michael Collins flew to the moon and back on July 16 through 24, 1969, just six months before the decade expired, thereby fulfilling President John F. Kennedy's challenge. Apollo 11 was the first of six lunar-landing missions (Apollos 11, 12, 14, 15, 16, 17) plus one mission abort (Apollo 13) launched between July, 1969, and December, 1972. It was during Apollo 11 that Neil Armstrong and Edwin E. Aldrin, Jr., became the first men to walk on the moon. The scarred heat shield and exterior are testimony to the enormous heat generated upon the command module's return through the earth's atmosphere when temperatures rose to over 5,000° F. during the 25,000-plus mph reentry speed. The command module *Columbia* also brought back to earth the first samples of lunar rocks and soil.

Only sixty-six years and about twenty feet separate the Apollo 11 command module from the Wright Flyer; this juxtaposition of two such epochal air- and spacecraft is not only indicative of the extraordinary technological advances flight has achieved in so short a time, but it is also an entirely appropriate expression of what the Smithsonian's National Air and Space Museum truly is.

A child's first tentative touch of a piece of the Moon.

The Apollo 11 command module Columbia, *which brought Neil Armstrong, Edwin Aldrin, and Michael Collins back from man's first walk on the Moon.*

Rocketry and Space Flight

The Rocketry and Space Flight gallery celebrates the realization of one of mankind's oldest dreams: to abandon his planet's confining sanctuary for voyages into space. It is ironic, however, that for much of the more than 2,000 years that man's dream was evolving, speculation on such travel could hold almost as many physical perils as the voyage itself.

When Galileo Galilei (1564 – 1642), the great Italian astronomer, mathematician, and physicist, focused his crude, newly invented telescope upon the heavens he discovered, among other things, how dangerous it could be to discuss what he had found. Mountains marching across a lunar landscape were fine. That the Milky Way was composed of thousands of millions of stars, that Saturn had rings, that the sun had spots, and that Venus went through phases like our Moon, all these discoveries by Galileo were safe, too. But when, on January 7, 1610, Galileo perceived four dimly lit bodies orbiting Jupiter, he had discovered a dangerous truth: that the speculations set forth a half-century earlier by the Polish astronomer Nicolaus Copernicus (1473–1543) in his *De Revolutionibus Orbium Coelestium* were correct. Copernicus' theory that the Sun was the center of a great system with the Earth and other planets revolving around it was so opposed to accepted beliefs and considered so "dangerous to the faith" that Copernicus dared not publish his treatise until near death. And even though Copernicus placatingly dedicated his work to the pope, Paul III, it was swiftly suppressed. Galileo's discovery sixty-seven years later of Jupiter's four moons, however, not only showed the validity of the Copernican Theory by proving that all heavenly bodies did not revolve around the Earth, even worse it indicated that if Jupiter had four moons to the Earth's mere one, then our planet might not even be of major importance in the celestial scheme.

The year before Galileo had turned his telescope on Jupiter, Johannes Kepler (1571–1630), the German astronomer and mathematician, had published the Danish astronomer Tycho Brahe's (1546–1601) precise and exacting calculations of the orbit of Mars, thus providing additional proof of the Copernican Theory. Kepler's work contained two of the three laws that now bear his name, which he had formulated on the rules governing planets' orbits. The first of Kepler's laws—that the orbit of each planet is an *ellipse* with the center of the Sun being one of its foci— would have surprised even Copernicus, who had supposed, as had the other astronomers, that a planet's orbit about the Sun would be a perfect circle. However, the theological grip on celestial science was still so strong that in 1633 Galileo was summoned to Rome, tried before the Inquisition, and imprisoned until forced to renounce upon oath any beliefs and writings that did not hold the Earth to be central to the universe with the Sun, planets, and stars in orbit about us.

A generation later Sir Isaac Newton (1642–1727), the English physicist and mathematician, came along "banishing,"

as Arthur C. Clarke has written,* "the last traces of metaphysics from the heavens, and turning the solar system into one vast machine whose every movement is explained by a single all-embracing law— the Law of Universal Gravitation." Newton's proof that no distinction exists between the rules governing the movement of the earth and those obeyed by every other celestial body destroyed forever the last vestiges of what Clarke calls "that closed and tidy medieval cosmos which contained only Heaven, earth and Hell like a three-story building." Astronomy ceased being a theological and philosophical science; it became instead an extension of the realm of mathematicians and geographers. Still, it would be almost three hundred more years before scientists and engineers would give serious thought to the realities of space flight. And when they did, they returned once more to Sir Isaac Newton, who, in 1687, had discovered and formulated the principle which accounts for how all rockets operate:

> To every action there is always opposed an equal reaction; or, the mutual actions of two bodies upon each other are always equal, and directed to contrary parts.

Visitors to the Rocketry and Space Flight gallery find rocket operation explained with illustrations from everyday life: when a frog jumps to shore from a chip of wood, the chip is propelled in the opposite direction. The force of the air escaping through the neck of an inflated balloon causes the balloon to dart about the room. A rocket is simply a device that creates a steady supply of gas to eject through a nozzle like the air from a balloon.

A rocket—a reaction-propelled device that carries both its own supply of fuel and the oxygen necessary to support combustion in airless space—is the only vehicle capable of

---

*Arthur C. Clarke and the Editors of "Life," *Man and Space*, Life Science Library, Time, Inc.

carrying man beyond the earth's atmosphere. And yet for many centuries the desire to travel in space and the technical development of the rocket engine proceeded along entirely separate paths, which did not converge until the twentieth century, when fantasy merged with technological fact. The divergence of these paths is illustrated as soon as the visitor enters the gallery where exhibits introduce both the history of the black-powder rocket and the dream of the first known science-fiction writer, the second-century A.D. Greek Lucian, whose book, *True History*, is the story of a fifty-man ship's company whose bark meets with a fierce Atlantic storm's whirlwind which picks them up and a week later deposits them on the Moon. There they encounter the cavalry of the Moon King, who ride into battle on three-headed buzzards; Windrunners, who are propelled into battle by the wind trapped within their great billowing shirts; salad birds, with lettuce leaf feathers, and so on. (Lucian was probably more a satirist poking fun at Homer's *Iliad* and *Odyssey* than a serious science-fiction writer.)

Exhibits trace China's discovery of gunpowder—an explosive mixture of potassium nitrate, sulfur, and charcoal, the earliest known recipe for which appeared in a Chinese volume written in A.D. 1040 — and its use in the thirteenth century in the first black-powder rockets. The evolution of the rocket from an incendiary arrow to a true war rocket is covered here. The second period exhibit deals with the fourteenth-century contributions to rocket technology from the Middle East. Included here is a model of the rocket-propelled "self-moving and combusting egg" first described by the Syrian scholar Hassan-er-Rammah in A.D. 1280. This weapon, powered by two black-powder rockets, contained an explosive or incendiary mixture in its flat pan and twin tails to direct it in a straight line through the water. It is uncertain whether such a device was ever built.

Another somewhat whimsical-looking

war machine appears in the third period exhibit: seventeenth-century Europe. It is Giovanni di Fontana's rocket-propelled ram for use against fortresses and other defensive works. A modified version was proposed for use against ships; neither was actually constructed. Fontana's *Bellicorum Instrumentorum Liber*, published in 1420, preceded by some fifty years Leonardo da Vinci's (1452–1519) famous war-machine sketches; and, in addition to a ram, Fontana proposed a rocket-propelled pigeon, hare, and fish. All three devices were incendiary weapons. Although the early use of rockets in the seventeenth century is covered in this exhibit, the technological advances made in rocketry were considerably less significant than the advances achieved in the sciences and, here, the gallery visitor is presented with the theories proposed by Copernicus, Brahe, Kepler, and Galileo.

Ironically, the rocket as a war weapon had, by the eighteenth century, been rendered obsolete by the development of more accurate and effective artillery. While improvements in rocket propellants and design continued, the emphasis was on firework displays and pyrotechnics, which had become increasingly popular forms of mass amusement.

The final exhibit in the Rocketry and Space Flight "corridor of history" concentrates on the re-emergence of the black-powder war rocket during the nineteenth century and its use in whaling and lifesaving. The nineteenth century is considered the "Golden Age" of black-powder rockets—although anyone familiar with *The Star Spangled Banner*'s "And the rockets' red glare, the bombs bursting in air, gave proof through the night that our flag* was still there…" knows that all that

---

*This very flag observed by Francis Scott Key, which flew over Baltimore Harbor's Fort McHenry throughout the British bombardment, is on exhibit in the Smithsonian Institution's National Museum of History and Technology.

glittered during that age was not gold. Sir William Congreve (1772–1828), having been impressed by the rockets used against the English in India, began a series of experiments in 1804 that led to the development of a metal-case stick-guided rocket capable of being fired in large barrages against enemy troop concentrations and fortifications. Congreve rockets played an important role during the War of 1812 and were used in many engagements against the Americans.

Toward the end of the nineteenth century science fiction and science fact began to merge. The French author Jules Verne, one of the most famous science-fiction writers of all time *(20,000 Leagues Under the Sea; Around the World in 80 Days; Journey to the Center of the Earth)*, wrote *From the Earth to the Moon* in 1865. Verne's tale, reflecting a careful blend of diligent scientific research, technical accuracy, prophetic vision, and sheer story-telling power, envisioned three men, a dog, and a couple of chickens, fired into lunar orbit from the Florida coast in a conical projectile by a 900-foot cannon. Their spacecraft was built for comfortable travel and decorated with the lavish appointments of the period.

Of course Verne's launching device with its 400,000 pounds of guncotton as a propellant charge would have eliminated his astronauts, but the author did correctly foresee the necessity of a 25,000-mph escape velocity to leave earth's gravity, that weightlessness would occur, that collisions with meteoroids were a possibility, and that their plush, upholstered "command module" could be steered by rockets in space. Two years later, in 1867, Verne retrieved his astronauts from permanent lunar orbit in the sequel, *Around the Moon*, and after bringing them through white-hot re-entry into earth's atmosphere, had their spacecraft splash down in the ocean.

By 1891, Hermann Ganswindt (1856–1934) was in Berlin drawing up

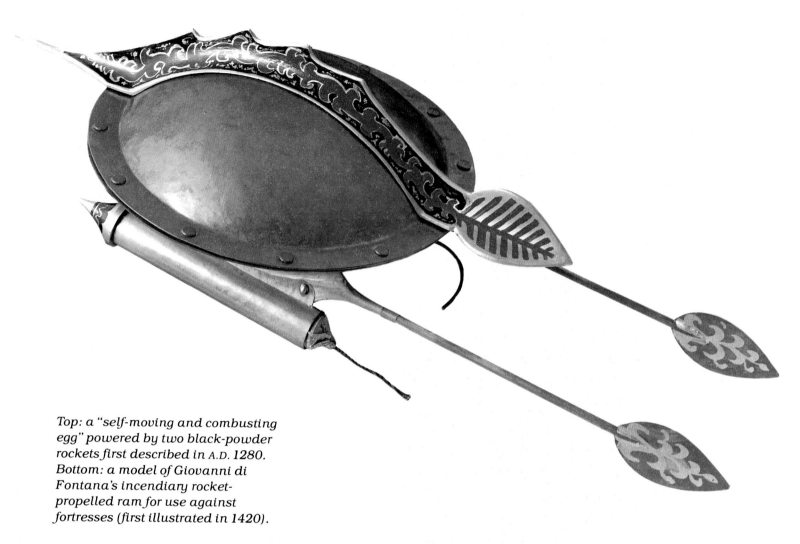

Top: a "self-moving and combusting egg" powered by two black-powder rockets first described in A.D. 1280. Bottom: a model of Giovanni di Fontana's incendiary rocket-propelled ram for use against fortresses (first illustrated in 1420).

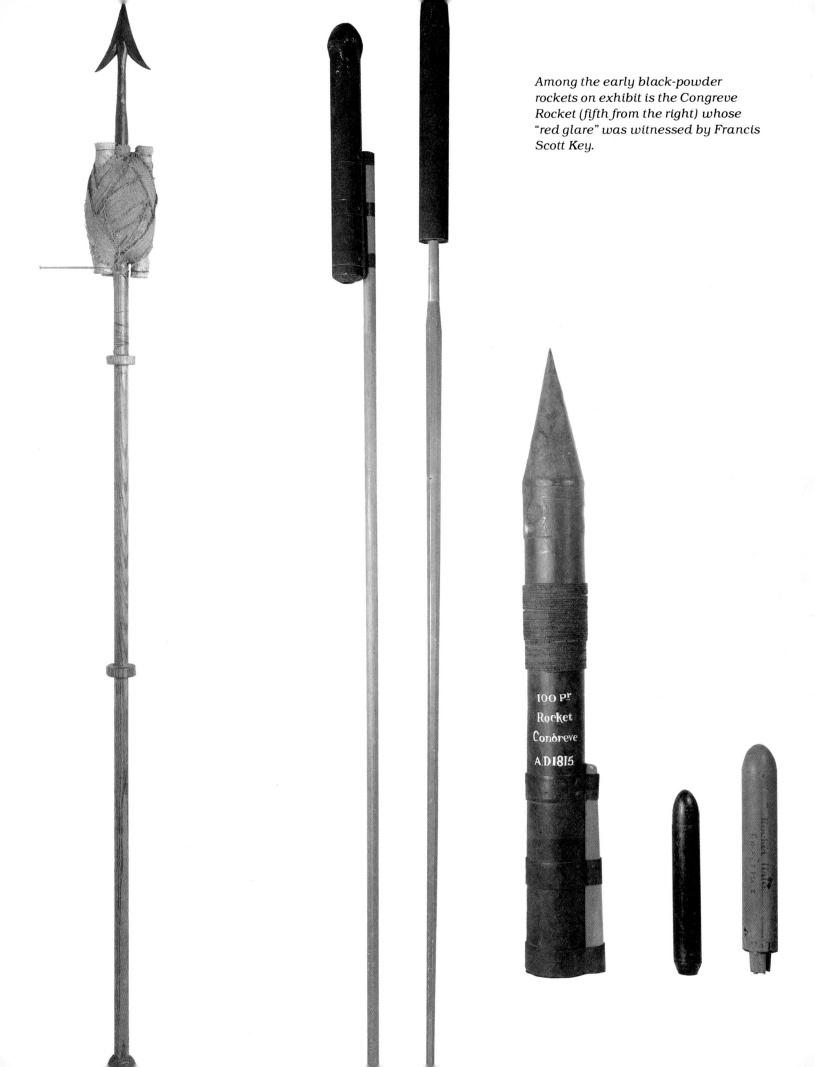

Among the early black-powder rockets on exhibit is the Congreve Rocket (fifth from the right) whose "red glare" was witnessed by Francis Scott Key.

100 Pr
Rocket
Congreve
A.D 1815.

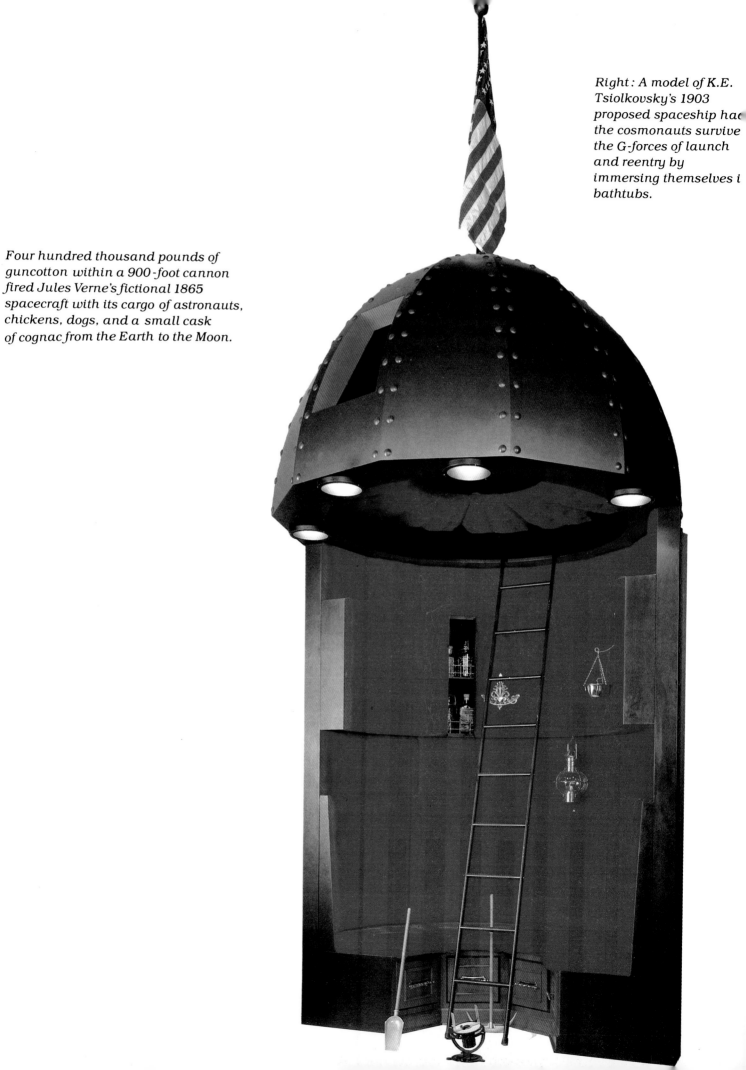

Four hundred thousand pounds of guncotton within a 900-foot cannon fired Jules Verne's fictional 1865 spacecraft with its cargo of astronauts, chickens, dogs, and a small cask of cognac from the Earth to the Moon.

Right: A model of K.E. Tsiolkovsky's 1903 proposed spaceship had the cosmonauts survive the G-forces of launch and reentry by immersing themselves in bathtubs.

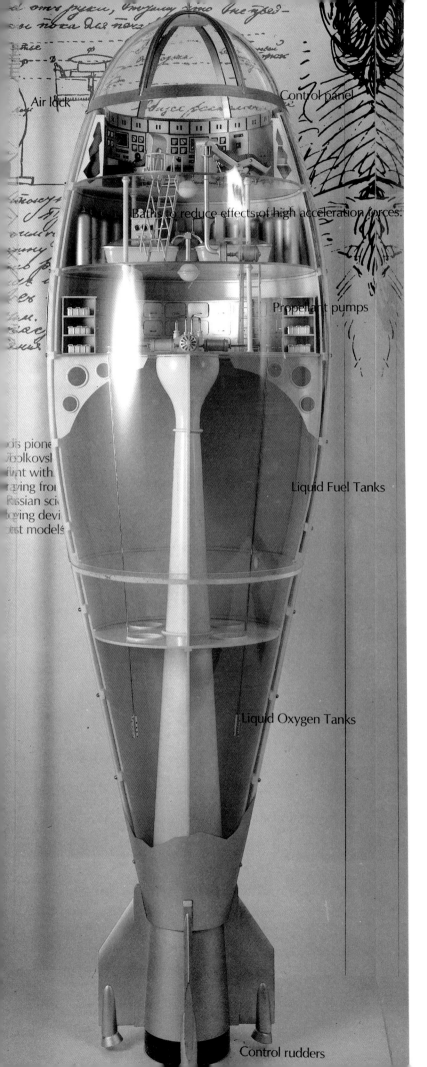

Air lock

Control panel

Baths to reduce effects of high acceleration forces.

Propellant pumps

Liquid Fuel Tanks

Liquid Oxygen Tanks

Control rudders

the first designs for a spaceship and demonstrating that solid-propellant rockets were the only means of getting man into space. In 1898, H.G. Wells published his classic *War of the Worlds*, which described a Martian invasion of Earth. This story formed the basis of Orson Welles' legendary October 31, 1938, Mercury Theater of the Air broadcast, which so terrified radio listeners that hundreds fled their homes believing the Martians had actually landed.

As the NASM visitor leaves the "corridor of history" the two divergent threads—the science and technology of rocket flight, and the desire to travel in space—at last converge and the twentieth century commences with Tsiolkovsky, Oberth, and Goddard, the three great pioneers of astronautics who laid the foundations for space flight.

Konstantin Eduardovitch Tsiolkovsky (1857–1935) was a self-educated Russian schoolteacher who, in 1903, published his now-classic article, "Exploration of Space with Reactive Devices," a theoretical study of rocket fuels and rocket-motor efficiency. Although he did not experiment with rocket engines, Tsiolkovsky showed why rockets would be necessary for space travel and proposed liquid hydrogen and liquid oxygen as the most efficient propellants. He conducted the first studies that demonstrated that space travel was, at least, theoretically possible and advanced the concept of multistage rockets. By 1903 Tsiolkovsky had also given careful thought to manned-spacecraft design and his description of such a ship demonstrates how completely fact and fantasy had by this time merged:

> Let's imagine the following configuration: a metal elongated chamber (having forms of least resistance), provided with its own light, oxygen, with absorbers of carbon dioxide, noxious effluvia and other animal excretions, intended not only for the maintenance of various physical devices, but also to provide life support to the men controlling the chamber.... The chamber contains a large supply of

Dr. Goddard's 1928 "hoopskirt" rocket (left) with propellant tanks on legs of frame; and (right) the rocket of May 4, 1926, which Goddard had modified to the now-classic design configuration of motor at rear surmounted by liquid oxygen and gasoline propellant tanks.

materials which, when combined, immediately form an explosive mass.

Tsiolkovsky proposed dividing his spaceship into three bays. The top bay in the rocket's nose housed the crew. Here would be the control panels, automatic instruments, decompression chambers, and comfortable couches. The second bay contained the oxygen supply and the "bathtubs" filled with water in which the crew members would immerse themselves to ease the powerful G-forces experienced during the rocket's launch and re-entry. The third bay housed the pumps necessary to move the propellants from the fuel tanks to the engine. The fuel tanks were below this third bay and would contain, Tsiolkovsky suggested, a liquid hydrocarbon and liquid oxygen.

To remain in orbit a spacecraft must achieve a speed of 18,000 mph, to escape gravity 25,000 mph. Even using hydrogen as a fuel, a rocket's exhaust could not exceed about 8,000 mph. By 1898 Tsiolkovsky had already asked the fundamental question upon whose answer all space flight depended: could one build a rocket that could fly faster than its own exhaust gases? Tsiolkovsky published his results in 1903, the year the Wright Flyer stumbled into the air under its own power. Tsiolkovsky's equation showed that up to the speed of light (670 million mph) there is no limit to the speed rockets can reach. The one major limiting factor was that at least 75 percent of a rocket's weight had to be its fuel. Nearly 400 years before Tsiolkovsky advocated the use of multistage rockets, an artillery officer, Conrad Haas, had proposed the same idea with black-powder rockets; Tsiolkovsky, however, suggested that the staging should be set up on a principle similar to an aircraft jettisoning its empty wing tanks. K.E. Tsiolkovsky died in 1935 an honored hero of the Soviet Union and was given a state funeral. One is impressed even today by Tsiolkovsky's vision of space exploration as an inevitable process that would transform and spread human life throughout the solar system.

"Earth is the cradle of the mind," Tsiolkovsky wrote, "but one cannot live in the cradle forever."

Hermann Oberth, another of the great astronautic pioneers, was, like Tsiolkovsky, a schoolteacher. Born in Transylvania (now central Rumania) in 1894, Oberth was fascinated by his childhood reading of Jules Verne's Moon books. In 1923, largely at his expense, Oberth published his own slim volume in Munich. This book, *The Rocket into Interplanetary Space,* was a serious attempt to demonstrate the theoretical possibility of space flight as well as to formulate its basic mathematics. In addition to proposing designs for man-carrying spacecraft and high-altitude research rockets, Oberth advanced the concept of orbital rendezvous for refueling and resupply by reviving the idea of orbiting a space station or large satellite—an idea first suggested in an 1870 *Atlantic Monthly* magazine fiction serial, "The Brick Moon," written by the Boston clergyman Edward Everett Hale.[*] Oberth was, like Tsiolkovsky, a theoretician, but his book excited the imagination of many young men who banded together to form rocket societies in America, Germany, and the Soviet Union and inspired that generation of engineers who actually built the rockets that would carry man into space. Oberth worked in the German rocket program during World War II, but came to this country afterward, and in 1955 joined the staff of America's Redstone Arsenal.

The only one of the three great pioneers to actually build and fly rockets was Robert H. Goddard, who was born in Worcester, Massachusetts, in 1882. Goddard was a quiet man who loved music, painting, and nature; a schoolteacher like Oberth and

---

[*]A prolific writer of magazine articles, Hale is perhaps best known for his short novel *The Man Without a Country.* From 1903 until his death in 1909 he was chaplain for the U.S. Senate. Hale's satellite was launched by a spinning flywheel.

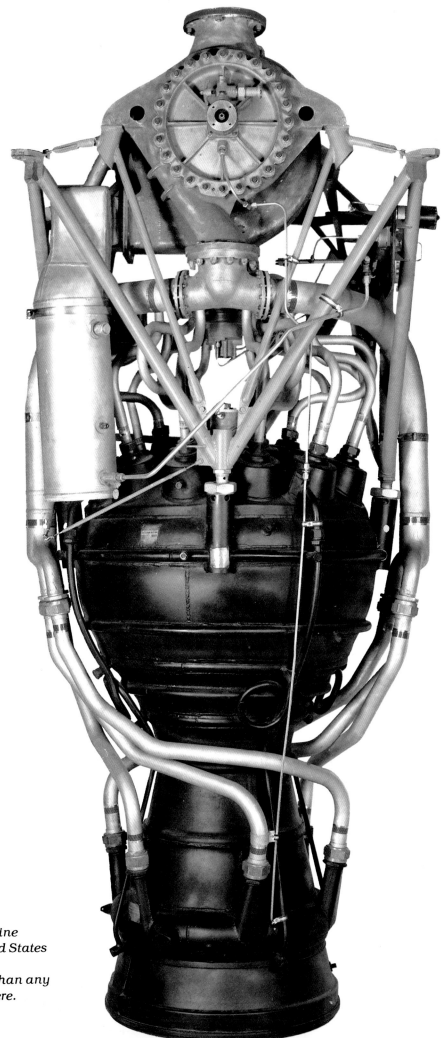

The V-2 rocket engine
made in the United States
after World War II
was much larger than any
previously built here.

The RL-10 upper-stage
propulsion unit powered the
Centaur stage that boosted
the Surveyor and Viking
craft into space.

45

Robert H. Goddard, at the blackboard at Clark University, in 1924, outlines for his students the problems of reaching the Moon by rocket.

Tsiolkovsky, he not only independently worked out the physical principles and calculations on rocketry and space flight, but went on to construct the world's first working liquid-fuel rockets.

Every visitor to the National Air and Space Museum probably knows who Orville and Wilbur Wright were and has some idea of the effects their invention has had on everyday life, but few of them realize that as a result of Robert Goddard's genius an immeasurably greater impact will be made on the lives of their children and generations yet unborn. The Wrights' invention has enabled us to race across our planet; Goddard's has made it possible for us to speed into space. As rocket expert Jerome Hunsaker said, "Every liquid-fuel rocket that flies is a Goddard rocket."

Just as Hermann Oberth had been inspired by his childhood reading of Jules Verne, Goddard's childhood reading of H.G. Wells' *The War of the Worlds* had enormous influence on him. By the age of seventeen, Goddard was already giving serious thought to rocketry and space flight. Goddard's studies of various rocket fuels while majoring in physics at Worcester's Clark University led him to conclude that the most effective propellant would be a combination

of liquid hydrogen and liquid oxygen—neither of which was then commercially available. Upon completing his doctorate in physics, Goddard began teaching at Clark, where his lectures in conventional physics also contained speculations upon methods of traveling in space. His suggested use of rockets as a means of reaching the Moon was included in a monograph entitled "A Method of Reaching Extreme Altitudes," published in 1919 by the Smithsonian Institution. The Smithsonian had granted $5,000 to Goddard for rocket research in 1917.

Goddard was ridiculed by the press, which called him "The Moon Man," and the *New York Times* derided him in an editorial for lacking "the knowledge daily ladled out in high schools." Mary Pickford, then a twenty-six-year-old movie starlet known as "America's Sweetheart," asked to be able to send a message in that first rocket to be launched to the Moon.

The Smithsonian provided the primary funding for Goddard's research from 1917 through 1929, during which period Goddard, who had early on recognized that liquid fuels provided a higher exhaust velocity than solid fuels, had been concentrating on developing a liquid-fuel rocket capable of carrying meteorological instruments to altitudes higher than those achieved by balloons. On March 16, 1926, after several successful static-fire tests, Robert Goddard launched his—and the *world's*—first liquid-propellant rocket. In his report to the Smithsonian's C.G. Abbot, Goddard wrote:

> In a test made March 16, out of doors, with a model...weighing 5¾ lb empty and 10¼ loaded with liquids, the lower part of the nozzle burned through and dropped off, leaving, however, the upper part intact. After about 20 sec. the rocket rose without perceptible jar, with no smoke and with no apparent increase in the rather small flame, increased rapidly in speed, and after describing a semi-circle, landed 184 feet from the starting point—the curved path being due to the fact that the nozzle had burned through unevenly, and one side was longer than the

The LR-87 gimbal-mounted twin-chambered, liquid-propellant rocket engine used to power the Titan I ICBM developed 300,000 pounds of thrust.

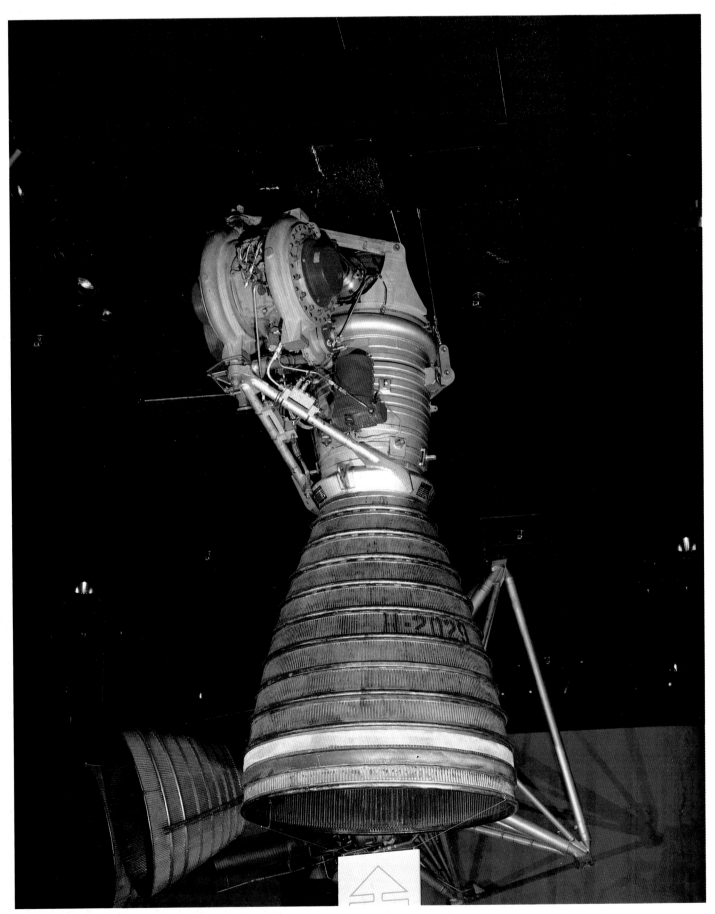

Foreground: The H-1 liquid-propellant rocket engine was used in the 8-engine cluster of the first stage of the Saturn I and IB launch vehicles. This engine was used in the launch of the U.S. crew of the Apollo-Soyuz Test Project. Background: The LR-87.

Three of these gold-plated vernier engines were used to soft-land the Surveyor spacecraft on the Moon. The engine's thrust could be varied from 30 to 104 pounds.

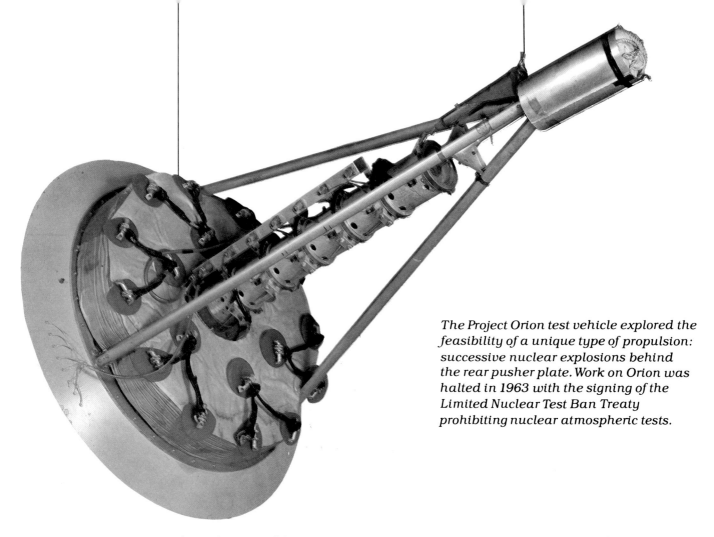

The Project Orion test vehicle explored the feasibility of a unique type of propulsion: successive nuclear explosions behind the rear pusher plate. Work on Orion was halted in 1963 with the signing of the Limited Nuclear Test Ban Treaty prohibiting nuclear atmospheric tests.

other. The average speed, from the time of the flight measured by a stopwatch, was 60 mph. This test was very significant as it was the first time that a rocket operated by liquid propellants travelled under its own power.

—"Robert H. Goddard and the Smithsonian Institution," by Frederick C. Durant III

The reason that Goddard's rocket lingered twenty seconds upon the test stand was that the rocket weighed more than its thrust of 9 pounds, and until the motor had expended enough fuel so that the rocket weighed less, its thrust could not lift it. The movie camera held by Goddard's wife, Esther, who was attempting to record this historic event for posterity, contained only seven seconds of film. The film, of course, had been expended before the rocket left the ground. "It looked almost magical as it rose without any appreciably greater noise or flame," Goddard enthusiastically reported, "as if it said, 'I've been here long enough; I think I'll be going somewhere else.'" Where the rocket went was 41 feet high into the air and, although it

traveled "down-range" only 184 feet, the flight of Goddard's rocket was every bit as significant as Wilbur and Orville Wright's first flight.

Throughout the 1920s Goddard continued rocket tests at his Aunt Effie's farm outside Worcester, but at times the Smithsonian could not hide its disappointment at his results. Once, upon receipt of a Goddard progress report in which the physicist had speculated about space travel, Abbot responded, "Interplanetary space travel would look much nearer to me after I had seen one of your rockets go up five or six miles in our own atmosphere." In May, after another flight with his March 16th rocket design, Goddard changed the configuration, placing the motor in the now-classic position at the rocket's base. This particular rocket, referred to as the May, 1926, device, is on display in this gallery. A replica of the original March 16, 1926, rocket in its first configuration is on display in the Milestones of Flight gallery.

Goddard was aware that he needed some

sort of spectacular success, and to achieve that he needed a much larger rocket. In 1927 he built a rocket with a 200-pound thrust, but it could not lift its weight. "Instead of a little flier," Esther Goddard said, "he had built a big sitter." Goddard decided to compromise. A medium-size rocket in the 40-pound-thrust range would reduce both construction effort and cost. Components could easily be designed and replaced. Goddard bought a secondhand windmill frame from a farmer and modified it as a launching tower for his 1928 "Hoop Skirt" rocket. Although the hoop was designed to add stability to the rocket's flight, the hoop kept getting caught in the launching tower. The rocket did finally fly, however, and reached an altitude of 90 feet. Flights were so noisy that in July, 1929, police, ambulances, and, unfortunately, reporters showed up at Aunt Effie's farm, where the tests were being carried out. One newspaper, with that blend of malice and glee which aviation pioneers had come to expect, headlined: MOON ROCKET MISSES TARGET BY 238,799½ MILES. Goddard was forbidden to make any more tests on the farm; but with the Smithsonian's assistance, he was able to work on his rockets at the United States Army artillery range at Fort (then Camp) Devens, Massachusetts.

In November, 1929, Goddard was visited by an important figure: Charles A. Lindbergh. Lindbergh, impressed by the potential of rocket power, suggested that his good friend and strong supporter of the fledgling aeronautic science, Daniel Guggenheim, help sponsor Goddard's work. Goddard soon received a two-year $50,000 grant from the Guggenheims and, at about the same time, the Smithsonian received $5,000 from the Carnegie Institute to further Goddard's research.

With the Guggenheim funding, Goddard was at last able to devote himself full-time to developing all the various elements of the sounding-rocket design he was working on. In 1930 he moved to Mescalero Ranch in Eden Valley near Roswell, New Mexico, where the climate, the landscape, and the privacy

were perfect for his work. There in Eden Valley, Goddard set up a permanent test facility and with his crew (which never numbered more than seven: Goddard's brother-in-law, Albert W. Kisk, and Henry Sachs, instrument makers; Charles Mansur and his brother, Lawrence, machinists; Nils T. Ljungquist, another instrument maker; Goddard himself, and his wife, Esther, who, in addition to being the official photographer, was also responsible for dousing fires caused by rocket exhausts) he conducted his research on rocket power plants, pumps, fuel systems and control mechanisms, which included gyrostabiliza-tion, steering jet vanes in the rocket exhaust, and aerodynamic flaps. The rocket had to be almost entirely handmade:

> Goddard ordered materials from large, hardware mail-order houses and his crew prowled through hardware stores, sporting-goods displays and auto-parts outlets. When they found something that might do a particular job—a child's wristwatch, a length of piano wire, an automobile sparkplug—they proceeded to use it to perform a function undreamed of by its manufacturers.
>
> A good deal of time had to be spent in the shop salvaging rockets that were successful—that is, they flew. A rocket that would not take off was a disappointment—but the rocket was usually left intact. A successful flight meant jubilation—and often carrying home a hunk of junk, all that remained after a crash landing. The smashed rockets could seldom be rebuilt, so Goddard designed and built a rocket recovery system with parachutes to ensure soft landings.
> —*Man and Space*, by Arthur C. Clarke and the Editors of "Life"

In 1932, two years after Goddard had set up his test facility in Roswell, New Mexico, the Guggenheim funds dried up because of the worldwide financial depression. Goddard returned to teaching at Clark University. He even had to ask the Smithsonian for $250 so that he could perform special tests concerned with reducing rocket weight.

In 1934, when the Guggenheim funding was resumed, Goddard still had to turn to the Smithsonian for assistance on specific problems and, in recognition of his very special relationship with the Smithsonian, Goddard, at the urging of Harry Guggenheim and Charles Lindbergh, sent the Institution a complete 1935 A-Series rocket—with the understanding that it not be exhibited until either he requested it or, in the event of his death, at the request of Lindbergh and Guggenheim. When the rocket arrived, its crate was bricked up inside a false wall within the Smithsonian and not exhumed until after World War II. This rocket is on display in the Satellites gallery.

Goddard was a gifted, ingenious engineer and an experienced and responsible scientist. During the Roswell years, 1930–40, and with but a small staff, Goddard built rocket engines and systems years ahead of their time. Among the many pioneering steps Goddard accomplished en route to successful liquid-propellant rocket-powered flight were the following: he obtained important performance data through static tests which enabled him to continually improve his designs; he pioneered gas-generator-powered, turbo-pump-fed rockets; he developed automatic launch-sequence control; he developed timed sequential actuation of tank pressurization, ignition, umbilical release, automatic shut-down, thrust determination, vehicle release, among others. Goddard also engineered on-board controls for guidance and engine shut-down, systems for parachute and payload recovery, and pioneered gyrostabilization and in-flight aerodynamic and rocket-exhaust deflection controls, as well as gimbal-mounted rocket motors. He developed recording and optical-telescopic tracking systems. And finally, he established a remarkable safety record throughout the Roswell period. Despite working with highly combustible and potentially dangerous propellants, there was not one serious accident during the innumerable static tests and thirty-one launches.

During World War II, Goddard left New Mexico for Annapolis, Maryland, to work for the government and developed Jet-Assisted Take-Off engines (JATO) for the Navy. In March, 1945, Goddard saw captured German V-2 Rocket parts for the first time. Although Goddard and the team of German scientists had worked separated not only by an ocean but by that theoretically most insurmountable of barriers, rigid wartime secrecy, Goddard saw that the V-2 rocket, though much larger than his latest model, used many similar systems. As Dr. Walter R. Dornberger, head of the German V-2 rocket team, explained, "That was the only way to build a rocket." But when, in 1950, Wernher von Braun, the German scientist who had presided over the V-2's development, examined the more than 200 patents Goddard was granted covering almost every aspect of liquid-fuel rockets, he said, "Until 1936, Goddard was ahead of us all."

Robert H. Goddard died in August, 1945. In his unpublished papers Goddard speculated about flights to the Moon, the planets, and beyond. He never outgrew the dream of that small boy who had read H.G. Wells' *War of the Worlds* and been struck with wonder at the challenge of the unknown. In 1932, Goddard wrote H.G. Wells a letter that said something important about his dream:

> How many more years I shall be able to work on the problem, I do not know; I hope, as long as I live. There can be no thought of finishing, for "aiming at the stars" both literally and figuratively, is a problem to occupy generations, so that no matter how much progress one makes, there is always the thrill of just beginning.

> —"Robert H. Goddard and the Smithsonian Institution," by Frederick C. Durant III

When the visitor leaves that part of the gallery devoted to Goddard's work he sees exhibits tracing the development of the different national rocket societies of the 1920s and 1930s, and from there he is

Right: Despite the problems of restricted mobility and poor stowage qualities, this RX-1 suit, on at least one occasion, kept a man alive and working on simulated tasks in a pressure environment like that of space.

Far right: This type of suit, worn by the astronauts on all Project Mercury flights, was designed to serve as an emergency backup system in case of cabin decompression.

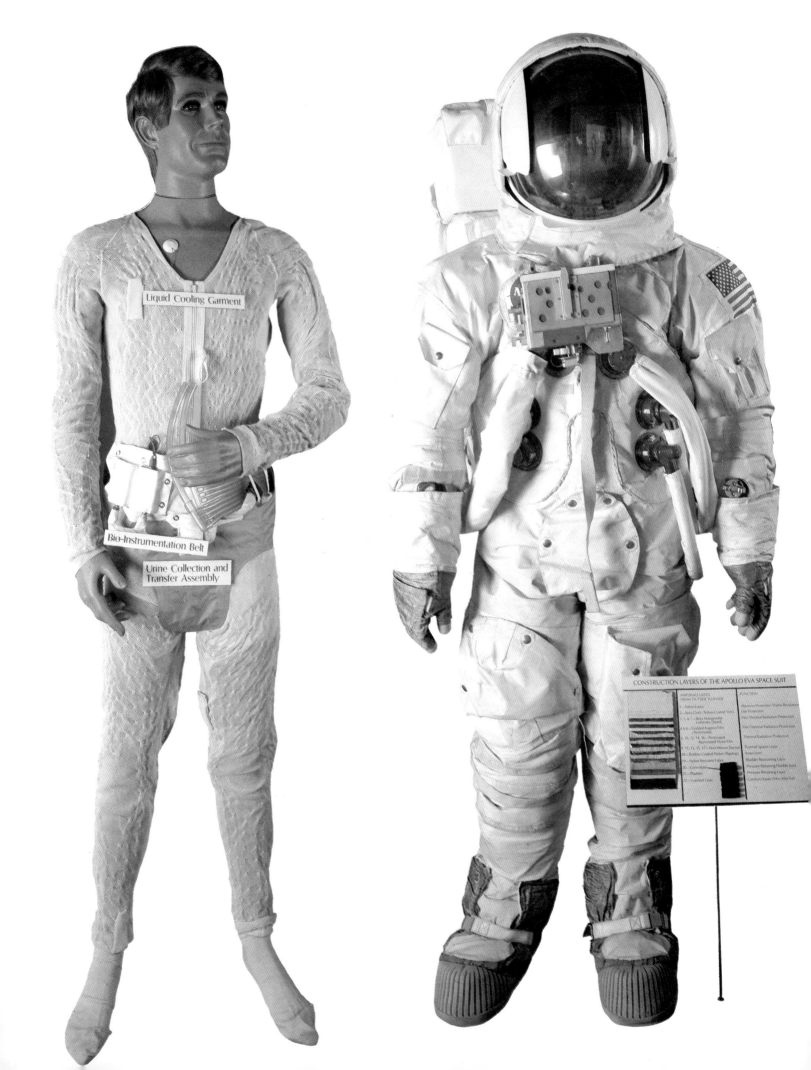

Liquid Cooling Garment

Bio-Instrumentation Belt

Urine Collection and
Transfer Assembly

CONSTRUCTION LAYERS OF THE APOLLO EVA SPACE SUIT

introduced to some of the larger rocket motors. The largest motors exhibited here are the RL-10 and the LR-87.

The RL-10 has an upper-stage propulsion system that can be stopped and restarted in space. RL-10s pioneered the use of liquid hydrogen as a rocket fuel and powered the Centaur launch vehicles that boosted crafts such as the Surveyor and Viking into space. A cluster of six RL-10 engines propelled the second stage of the Saturn I rocket. The RL-10 exhibited here has been cut away so that the visitors can see the "plumbing" inside and gain some understanding of how the rocket works.

The LR-87 was a twin-chamber liquid-propelled rocket engine developed for the Titan I intercontinental ballistic missile. The combustion chambers are gimbal-mounted so that the exhaust could be swiveled to direct the missile's trajectory during the powered phase of flight. One of the most fascinating exhibits here is the display area set aside for the sounds the various rockets made.

When the visitor completes his tour of Rocketry and Space Flight he enters the final area of this gallery, where he is introduced to the development of the space suit.

As man ventures out of his Earth's environment it is obvious that he must carry his "environment" with him. As his craft climbs away from Earth, the atmospheric pressure gradually diminishes until it disappears entirely. Beyond 40,000 feet, the limit for unpressurized flight, lungs no longer absorb sufficient oxygen to replenish the bloodstream; beyond 460,000 feet the atmosphere no longer provides protection against micrometeoroids. Were the pilot's pressure suit to be punctured by micrometeroids, death would rapidly follow;

therefore, several layers of plastic protect the pressure-retaining layer of the suit.

Pressure-suit development was an inevitable outgrowth of international competition for altitude and speed records. Since many of the problems confronting the man in the thin upper reaches of the atmosphere would be the same as for a man in the depths of the sea, the first pressure suits resembled deep-sea diving suits more than "space suits," a resemblance already familiar to the visitor who saw, in the Flight Testing gallery, the world's first practical flight pressure suit worn by Wiley Post. There is a difference between pressure suits and "space suits," however. Both space suits and pressure suits need to provide protection, mobility, comfort, and minimum bulk at light weight. In addition, the space suit must make provision for micrometeoroid protection, waste management, and the extreme temperatures of space. Consider, for example, the fact that the Apollo space suit worn during the walk on the Moon would be alternately exposed to temperatures on the surface of +250° F. in the sun and −200° F. in shadow. The astronaut's portable life-support system (PLSS) had to create and maintain a livable atmosphere inside the space suit. The PLSS could be worn for seven hours without being recharged. It supplied oxygen for breathing purposes, suit pressurization, communication, and ventilation. It also supplied cool water and oxygen for body cooling and removed contaminants from the oxygen circulating through the suit. Fully charged, the pack weighed 104 pounds. Fortunately, because of the lower gravity, the pack weighed but 17 pounds on the Moon.

The visitor to this gallery might be amused by the exhibits showing the at times startling similarity between the space suits worn by the astronauts and those proposed by cartoonists and early science-fiction writers; but he should also come away from this gallery with an appreciation that what was science fiction yesterday is fact today. And, in like manner, what is science fiction today will tomorrow be reality.

Far left: A layered liquid cooling garment that provides for body cooling.
Left: Designed and created primarily for Moon walking, this suit, with its backpack, enabled the lunar astronauts to dispense with the tether-umbilical used on the Pioneer-Gemini "spacewalks" and to roam free over the lunar surface. The development of this space suit system was one of the most complex elements in the history of manned space flight.

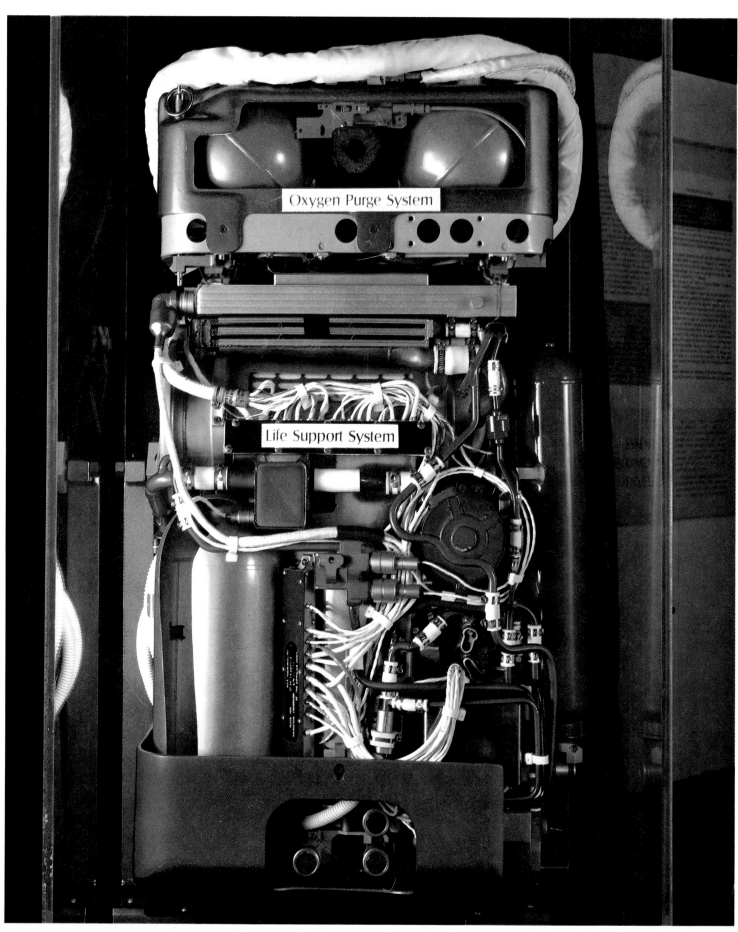

*The fully charged 104-pound Apollo Portable Life Support System (PLSS)
fortunately weighed but 17 pounds on the 1/6 Earth gravity of the Moon.*

Satellites

On September 21, 1938, a major eastern metropolitan newspaper editorial entitled "Hurricane" concluded that the reason most of the East Coast was able to keep abreast of a hurricane's path was due to "an admirably organized meteorological service" that with the help of all the ships in the Caribbean keeps an hourly watch on the cyclone "peril that it is, until at last it whirls out into the Atlantic . . . ."

The very morning the editorial appeared a tropical hurricane off Cape Hatteras and the Carolinas that was expected to "whirl out into the Atlantic" instead suddenly and freakishly veered north without warning and raced 600 miles in 12 hours, picking up speed to shatter the unsuspecting East Coast of the United States from New York to Boston with such ferocity that it was later called the worst natural disaster in American history. Winds of 186 mph were recorded at the Harvard Observatory; at least 680 lives were lost, 708 persons injured; property damage was over $400 million; 4,500 summer cottages and farm buildings were destroyed, 15,139 were damaged; 26,000 automobiles were smashed, 2,605 boats were lost; 275 million trees were broken off or uprooted.* Along the coasts of Connecticut and Rhode Island, high tide rose from 12 to 25 feet above mean low water, inundating the land and washing buildings out to sea; most of the storm's victims in Rhode Island and Cape Cod were carried away by a huge

---

*For comparison, 450 lives were lost during the 1906 San Francisco earthquake and fire and $350 million property damage occurred; in the Great Chicago Fire of 1871, 200 lives were lost and $200 million property damage was estimated.

tidal wave. The following day the Associated Press reported, "The greens and commons of New England will never be the same. Picture postcard mementos of the oldest part of the United States are gone with the wind and the flood. The day of the 'biggest wind' has just passed and a great part of most picturesque America, as old as the Pilgrims, has gone beyond recall or replacement."

Today, of course, with meteorological satellites such as Tiros aloft, hourly tracking of such a storm would be possible. Warning would be given, lives would be saved, although the now even more crowded shoreline would, nevertheless, be devastated again. The application of satellites for weather observation, however, came almost as an unexpected by-product of their intended scientific employment: to gather information on the nature of the atmosphere and near-earth environment.

Our ancestors in the world of centuries past certainly wondered about and feared the strange and terrifying mysteries that filled the air—the awesome winds, the terrible blizzards, the savage thunderstorms and lightning. And, too, they must have marveled at the exquisite beauty of rainbows, sunsets, the mysterious northern lights. What caused these strange phenomena? Where did they come from? What did they mean? By the sixteenth century, scientists had developed instruments capable of investigating some of these mysteries—the atmosphere's temperature, its composition, how and why it moved—but they needed a means of raising their instruments high into the sky. They experimented with kites of different sorts and sizes, but a kite could go only as

The dizzying "Satellite Array" suggests how crowded near-Earth space has become.

high as the length of its string. Balloons, which had started carrying passengers in the latter part of the eighteenth century, were used to lift scientists and their instruments as well. But by the nineteenth century, the danger of high-altitude flights in the thin, cold atmosphere and the difficulty of reading and operating instruments while suspended in an open basket beneath a bobbing balloon had become apparent, and even in the sealed gondolas of the twentieth century, the limitations of balloons capable of carrying scientists to the roof of the atmosphere for limited periods of time made themselves felt. Instruments were developed that functioned automatically, thus eliminating the need for a scientist to accompany them (instrumented balloons are still used today to gather long-term information on the lower atmosphere); but there continued to exist the need to go higher than balloons could reach. Robert H. Goddard's monograph, "A

Method of Reaching Extreme Altitudes," published by the Smithsonian in 1919, recognized that the rocket was the only vehicle capable of carrying scientific instruments to the upper reaches of the atmosphere and into space beyond the reach of balloons, kites or airplanes. The desire to gather information on the nature of the atmosphere and near-earth environment was one of the most important factors leading to the development of modern space technology. The earliest earth satellites represented a logical extension of existing sounding rocket programs.

The term "sounding" is derived from the seamen's centuries-long use of sounding lines to measure the depth of unknown waters. Sounding rockets were developed to provide scientists with a means of investigating and "measuring" the "unknown waters" of the atmosphere in a similar fashion. A 1935 Goddard A-Series rocket is displayed with sections of its skin removed, its parts labeled and explained.

Also on exhibit is an Aerobee-150 which can lift a 150-pound payload to an altitude of 170 miles. Aerobees did 99 percent of the early scientific and sensing work. Near the Aerobee-150 is a WAC Corporal which, when launched in 1944, was the first successful American sounding rocket to achieve a significant altitude: 235,000 feet when boosted atop a captured German V-2 rocket! There is a Viking which was used to measure air temperature, density, pressure, and composition and to provide data on cosmic and solar radiation; and a Nike-Cajun of the type used extensively during the International Geophysical Year (1957-58) to perform a number of research tasks such as weather photography, studies of water vapor distribution in the upper atmosphere, and magnetic soundings in the ionosphere. The final large rocket in this section is the curiously hybrid four-stage Farside, which was launched from a balloon as an extremely high-altitude research vehicle. This 2,000-pound, 24-foot-long rocket was positioned within an aluminum structure suspended directly beneath a huge polyethylene balloon. When the balloon carrying the Farside rocket achieved an altitude of 19 miles, the rocket was fired directly through the balloon, carrying the instrument payload to an estimated altitude of 4,000 miles to study cosmic rays, the earth's magnetic field, electromagnetic radiation in space, the presence of interplanetary gases, and the nature of meteoric dust.

Since many of the first satellites carried the same instruments to examine the same phenomena as their sounding rocket predecessors they were sometimes known as "long-playing rockets." The great advantage of a satellite over a rocket is obviously its ability to provide a continuous flow of information for an extended period of time. It soon became apparent, however, that an orbital platform not only could be used to investigate questions of interest to scientists, but that it could also provide novel solutions to problems in fields as diverse as communications, weather observation, navigation, and the monitoring of earth resources on a global scale. The earth satellite thereby became one of the most valuable instruments of the space age.

The successful orbiting by the Soviets on October 4, 1957, of the 184-pound Sputnik 1[*] dramatically demonstrated the advanced state of Soviet space technology and precipitated in the United States a sense of crisis and disbelief. The American public, which had not thought the Soviet Union had the technological expertise or capability for orbiting a satellite, believed the United States had suffered a humiliating defeat in an emerging "space race," which indeed it had. Just over a year before Sputnik, however, a rocket launched on September 20, 1956, by the United States Army from Cape Canaveral reached a speed of 13,000 mph and could easily have accelerated the remaining 5,000 mph necessary to have gone into orbit but

[*] The great Soviet space theoretician K. E. Tsiolkovsky first suggested naming an artificial earth satellite "sputnik," a word translated as "fellow traveler" or "traveling companion."

did not, according to Arthur C. Clarke,

> . . . for a reason that was as simple as it is hard to believe. The Department of Defense, suspecting (not without reason) that the Army might launch an unauthorized satellite and apologize later, had ordered that the last stage must be an empty dummy; Dr. Wernher von Braun was personally directed to make sure that this order was obeyed. Not until 16 months later—when two Russian satellites had already orbited—was he given an opportunity to launch an almost identical vehicle with a live final stage. That final stage was the first United States satellite, Explorer 1.

—*Man and Space*, by Arthur C. Clarke and the Editors of Life

It should be remembered that the United States Army's rocket program in 1956 was directed toward the development of ballistic missiles, not toward the launching of satellites. The official American satellite program was Project Vanguard—a non-military effort—that would rely on a launch vehicle specifically developed for that purpose. Project Orbiter, the competing Army plan, relied upon a modified Redstone missile, the exact specifications of which would have to be withheld from the world scientific community for security reasons. The Army was testing nose cones of intercontinental ballistic missiles; an orbiting warhead could be considered a form of nuclear blackmail, an overtly aggressive gesture during a period of intense international tensions.

Nineteen fifty-six was the year of the Hungarian uprising, the revolt of the Poznan workers in Poland, and the first Soviet congress since the death of Stalin, during which the Communist party chief, Nikita S. Khrushchev, stated, "We want to be friends and to cooperate with the United States in the effort for peace and security of the peoples as well as in the economic and cultural fields . . . ." It was also the year that a joint military action by Great Britain and France was directed against an Egyptian takeover of the Suez Canal, and that an American B-52 over the Bikini Atoll demonstrated that the United States had a

workable hydrogen bomb it could deliver anywhere in the world. In the weeks that followed the successful Soviet launch, work on Project Vanguard continued under great pressure, a pressure that was increased when, less than one month after the launch of Sputnik 1, the Russians orbited Sputnik 2—a 1,121-pound satellite containing a live dog, Laika—with its final more-than-five-ton rocket stage still attached! The first American satellite, a minuscule 3.3-pound Vanguard 1, was prepared for launch on December 6, 1957, from its Cape Canaveral pad. Kurt Stehling, the Vanguard propulsion engineer, described what happened when the launch countdown passed zero:

> It seemed as if all the gates of Hell had opened up. Brilliant stiletto flames shot out from the side of the rocket near the engine. The vehicle agonizingly hesitated a moment, quivered again, and in front of our unbelieving shocked eyes, began to topple. It also sank like a great flaming sword into its scabbard down into the blast tube. It toppled slowly, breaking apart, hitting part of the test stand and ground with a tremendous roar that could be felt and heard even behind the 2-foot concrete walls of the blockhouse.

—*Man and Space*, by Arthur C. Clarke and the Editors of Life

The grapefruit-sized Vanguard continued to beep pathetically even while it was being consumed by flames. The satellite was recovered and is now in the Apollo to the Moon gallery, displayed in the open hand of a dismayed-looking Uncle Sam.

Explorer 1, America's first successful satellite, a 30.8-pound device that was about 6½ feet long, counting its attached fourth stage of the rocket, was launched on January 31, 1958, atop a four-stage Jupiter-C rocket designed, built and fired by the Army Ballistic Missile Agency headed by Dr. Wernher von Braun.

Unfair criticism and the memory of the first launch disaster have obscured the record of real successes achieved by subsequent Vanguard vehicles—Vanguard 1, launched March 17, 1958, Vanguard 2, on

February 17, 1959, and Vanguard 3, on September 18, 1959—the technical achievements embodied in the launch vehicle, the creation of the important minitrack tracking system, the first use of silicon solar cells to provide electric power in a satellite, the discovery of the earth's pear shape, a survey of the earth's magnetic field, the location of the lower edge of the earth's radiation belts, and a wealth of new scientific data.

Visitors to the main exhibition area can learn what maintains a satellite in orbit; about orbital and escape velocities (18,000 mph for the former, 25,000 for the latter); about the variety of possible orbits, and the utility of particular orbital altitudes and inclinations; and the sorts of satellites that make use of particular orbits and why. Then, with an acquaintance with the fundamentals of satellite theory and history, the visitor can study at leisure the "Satellite Array," a dazzling grouping of satellites suspended from the gallery ceiling which almost inadvertently suggests how crowded near-space has become in the more than twenty years since Sputnik was launched.* The array also effectively demonstrates the great diversity in design for satellites used for different purposes. A circular rail beneath the satellites carries an illustration of the various satellites and describes their functions. There are scientific satellites of the Explorer series—a name which goes back to the 1930s before NASA was formed when Explorers were U.S. Army Air Service-National Geographic stratosphere balloons. The name, "Explorer," is indicative of the mission performed by the more than fifty satellites of this series: the exploration of the

unknown. Explorer 1, launched January 31, 1958, was the first successful American satellite. NASA used Explorers to study the atmosphere and ionosphere, the magnetosphere and interplanetary space, astronomical and astrophysical phenomena, and the earth's shape, magnetic field, and surface. Some of the various Explorers' descriptive designations show the many different kinds of scientific experiments and programs these satellites performed: Aeronomy Explorer; Air Density Satellite; Direct Measurement Explorer; Interplanetary Monitoring Platform (IMP); Ionosphere Explorer; Meteoroid Technology Explorer (MTE); Radio Astronomy Explorer (RAE); Solar Explorer; Small Astronomy Satellite (SAS).

The X-ray Astronomy Explorer is on exhibit in this gallery. Explorer 42, or SAS-A, launched on December 12, 1970 by an Italian crew from the San Marco platform off the coast of Kenya, Africa, was named *Uhuru* (Swahili for "freedom") because it was launched on Kenya's Independence Day. During its four years in orbit the small satellite mapped the universe in X-ray wavelengths, discovered X-ray pulsars and evidence of black holes.

Two Ariel satellites are also on exhibit here. Ariel-1, launched from Cape Canaveral on April 26, 1962, was the world's first international satellite. Ariel-1, the result of a cooperative project between the United Kingdom and NASA, was built by NASA's Goddard Space Flight Center and instrumented with six British experiments designed to make integrated measurements of the ionosphere, as well as other scientific observations.

There are three major kinds of Applications Satellites: Communications, Meteorological, and Earth Monitoring Satellites. *Early Bird* the first Intelsat (an acronym for *International Telecommunications Satellite* Organization which owns and operates these communications satellites) was launched by NASA on April 6, 1965 and placed in geosynchronous orbit

---

*By January, 1975, 1,740 payloads had been fired into space; of those, 1,007 have been destroyed reentering our atmosphere or by impacting on other worlds, 684 continue in orbit, and 49 are still drifting out into space. It has been estimated that the actual number of man-made objects floating about in space is closer to 4,600, which includes spent military boosters, broken transmitters, and bits and pieces of other machines.

over the Atlantic Ocean. Subsequent Intelsat satellites have enormously increased both in size and in communications capabilities. Intelsat 2 and Intelsat 3 are on exhibit here and the visitor can learn the historic evolution of these craft from the Echo balloon series to the creation of Intelsat and Comsat, and the modern global communications network.

Daily weather forecasts, storm warnings and scientific studies of weather dynamics are provided by the second category of Application Satellites—the Meteorological Satellites. On exhibit is a Tiros (*Television and Infra-Red Observation Satellite*). Tiros-1 was launched April 1, 1960; by early 1964 NASA had launched seven additional Tiros satellites capable of providing photographic coverage of about 20 percent of the earth's surface each day. A video terminal in the satellite bay, tied to the Goddard Space Flight Center, delivers a facsimile weather photo broadcast by the Synchronous Meteorological Satellite every half hour.

The exhibit pertaining to the third category of Applications Satellites, the Earth Resources Technology Satellites (or Earth Monitoring Satellites), is entirely graphic and contains a variety of satellite photos to explain how vehicles such as the Landsat and Seasat satellites contribute to the solution, understanding and location of pollution problems, mineral resources, crop surveillance (for the effects of drought, insects and disease), the impact of huge construction programs, strip-mining, forest fires, flood control, city planning, land use and mysteries spawned and unexplainable on the earth's surface but visible and, therefore solvable, from space.

A Biosatellite is exhibited with the parachute used during its recovery. Biosatellites were developed to conduct space experiments with living organisms, both plant and animal. Specimens in orbit underwent prolonged weightlessness, radiation and other conditions of the space environment thereby permitting scientists the opportunity to study the effects of space on various life processes prior to launching human beings.

As the visitor emerges from the gallery, he passes again a video display placed within a large viewing chamber. There a familiar-looking man sits behind a desk in a familiar network television newsroom. He is saying,

We have learned much from satellites and we have learned much about them—what they can do—what they cannot do—and what we can expect from them in the future. They are now exotic tools of science and communications—and their potential has only just begun to be realized. The satellites of the future—now little more than a gleam in an engineer's eye—will continue to return new knowledge from space and enable man to improve his condition on Earth in ways that most of us can't imagine. They are here to stay. [The sound of a teletype machine rises in the background.] And that's the way it is. This is Walter Cronkite.

Biosatellite 2 carried frog eggs, plants, microorganisms, and insects into orbit on September 7, 1967, to study the combined effects of weightlessness, radiation, and the absence of normal day-night cycles on biological processes. After two days in space, Biosatellite 2 re-entered the atmosphere and was caught in mid-air by an Air Force recovery aircraft.

Apollo to the Moon

I believe that this nation should commit itself to achieving the goal, before this decade is out, of landing a man on the moon and returning him safely to earth. No single space project in this period will be more impressive to mankind or more important for the long-range exploration of space. And none will be so difficult or expensive to accomplish.

—President John F. Kennedy, May 25, 1961

A videotape of the young President delivering this speech before a special joint session of Congress is one of the first images a visitor to the Apollo to the Moon gallery sees. President Kennedy's announcement that the United States intended to land a man on the Moon before the decade was out did more than define a new role for America's manned space flight program; it expressed in unequivocal terms this country's determination to win the space race, which had not only already clearly begun—but which also, just as clearly, America was already losing.

Three and a half years earlier, Sputnik's faint, otherworldly *beep-beep-beep* had stunned the American people and proven that the Soviet Union's scientific and technological capabilities were far advanced of what had been believed. Furthermore, the launching and successful orbiting of the 1,121-pound satellite Sputnik 2, several weeks later, indicated that the Soviet boast that they possessed intercontinental ballistic missiles capable of striking American cities was possibly true. To understand the significance of President Kennedy's challenge and how the lunar landing was to become a tangible symbol of this nation's

resolve to restore its lost prestige, it helps to recall the events that led up to the President's speech.

One successful Soviet space launch after another had placed increasingly massive payloads into orbit while, in the most publicized failure in history, America's 3.3-pound grapefruit-sized Vanguard satellite had plaintively whistled even as its rocket consumed itself in flames. The American people's growing frustration and humiliation as they watched their rockets explode on their launch pads had resulted in grave doubts not only about this nation's technological prowess, but about the whole educational process in the United States. And then, on April 12, 1961, just before the President's speech, the Russians had orbited Major Yuri A. Gagarin. And, five days later, there occurred the debacle of the Bay of Pigs. American morale could not have been lower.

In the fall of 1958, NASA had begun the process of selecting the astronauts and establishing the criteria for the sort of men they needed: the men would have to be pilots, engineers, explorers, scientists, guinea pigs; they would have to be physically strong enough to endure the stresses and requirements of space flight and emotionally strong enough to withstand the pressures and demands made upon them before and after their return. The men would have to have daring and courage, but above all would have to remain cool and resourceful in the face of unforeseen emergencies or hazards. NASA set their top age at 40 (there have since been changes); their height was to be no more than 5′11″* and weight no more than 180 pounds. NASA further announced that no applicant would be considered who did not have a formal engineering degree or its equivalent. NASA immediately turned to the ranks of practicing military test pilots on the theory that these men already had the sort of experience and credentials future astronauts would need. At 2 PM, on April 9, 1959, the seven men who had been selected were introduced to the press. When one of the reporters asked the astronauts who, among them, would be willing to go into space right then and there, all seven raised their hands. They were M. Scott Carpenter, L. Gordon Cooper, Jr., John H. Glenn, Jr., Virgil I. Grissom, Walter M. Schirra, Jr., Alan B. Shepard, Jr., and Donald K. Slayton. Two years after our astronauts' introduction to the press, Russia's Yuri Gagarin was launched into space. Alan Shepard in *Freedom 7* would follow Gagarin three weeks later, on May 5, 1961.

The morning Shepard was scheduled to become the first American in space, the launch of his *Freedom 7* Mercury spacecraft had been delayed by cloud cover and problems with a small inverter that needed to be replaced. Shepard and Grissom had been killing time in the van trying to relax. Prior to Gagarin's orbit, the Soviets had launched seven dogs into space, Laika (11/3/57), Strelka and Belka (8/19/60), Pshchelka and Mushka (12/1/60), Chernushka (3/9/61), and Zvezdochka (3/25/61), four of whom had survived. Shepard was listing the desired qualities for being an astronaut: courage, perfect vision, low blood pressure, coordination. "And you've got to

have four legs," Shepard said.

"Why four legs?" asked Grissom.

"They really wanted to send a dog," Shepard replied, "but they thought that would be too cruel."

About four hours later, Shepard was launched in *Freedom 7* atop a Redstone rocket that generated 78,000 pounds of thrust:

Just after the count of zero Deke [Slayton, seated at the Capsule Communicator desk at Mercury Control Center] said, "Lift-off." Then he added a final tension-breaker to make me relax. "You're on the way, José," he said.

I think I braced myself a bit too much while Deke was giving me the final count. Nobody knew, of course, how much shock and vibration I would really feel when I took off. There was no one around who had tried it and could tell me; and we had not heard from Moscow how it felt.…

There was a lot less vibration and noise rumble than I had expected. It was extremely smooth—a subtle, gentle, gradual rise off the ground.…But there was no question that I was going.…I could see it on the instruments, hear it on the headphones, feel it all around me.

It was a strange and exciting sensation. And yet it was so mild and easy—much like the rides we had experienced in our trainers—that it somehow seemed very familiar.…For the first minute the ride continued to be very smooth. My main job just then was to keep the people on the ground as relaxed and informed as possible.… So I did quite a bit of reporting over the radio about oxygen pressure and fuel consumption and cabin temperature and how the G's were mounting slowly, just as we had predicted they would.…

One minute after lift-off the ride did get a little rough. This was where the booster and the capsule passed from sonic to supersonic speed and then immediately went slicing through a zone of maximum dynamic pressure as the forces of speed and air density combined at their peak. The spacecraft started vibrating here. Although my vision was blurred for a few seconds, I had no trouble seeing the instrument panel. We had known that something like this was going to happen, and if I had sent down a garbled message that it was worse than we had expected and that I was really getting buffeted, I think I might have put everybody on the ground in a state of shock. I did not want to panic anyone into ordering me to leave. And I did not

---

*The reason for the height limitation was determined by the size of the Mercury spacecraft already on the drawing boards, whose dimensions, in turn, were dictated by the size of the available Redstone and Atlas boosters, which would launch the Mercury spacecraft into space. The diameter of the Mercury spacecraft at its base was 74″, or 6′2″. Once an astronaut was in his space suit and helmet, anyone taller than 5′11″ simply would not fit.

want to leave. So I waited until the vibration stopped and let the Control Center know indirectly by reporting to Deke that it was "a lot smoother now, a lot smoother."

... The engine cutoff occurred right on schedule, at two minutes and 22 seconds after lift-off. Nothing abrupt happened, just a delicate and gradual dropping off of the thrust as the fuel flow decreased. I heard a roaring noise as the escape tower blew off...and then I heard a noise as the little rockets fired to separate the capsule from the booster. This was a critical point of the flight, both technically and psychologically. I knew that if the capsule got hung up on the booster, I would have quite a different flight, and I had thought about this possibility quite a lot before lift-off....Right after leaving the booster, the capsule and I went weightless together and I could feel the capsule begin its slow, lazy turnaround to get into position for the rest of the flight. It turned 180 degrees, with the blunt or bottom end swinging forward now to take up the heat....The capsule was traveling at about 5,000 miles per hour now....All through this period, the capsule and I remained weightless. And though we had had a lot of free advice on how this would feel—some of it rather dire—the sensation was...pleasant and relaxing. It had absolutely no effect on my movements or my efficiency. I was completely comfortable, and it was something of a relief not to feel the pressure and weight of my body against the couch. The ends of my straps floated around a little, and there was some dust drifting around in the cockpit with me. But these were unimportant and peripheral indications that I was at Zero G.

... At five minutes and 14 seconds after launch, the first of the three [retro-]rockets went off, right on schedule. The other two went off at the prescribed five-second intervals. There was a small upsetting motion as our speed was reduced, and I was pushed back into the couch a bit by the sudden change in Gs. But each time the capsule started to get pushed out of its proper angle by one of the retros going off I found I could bring it back again with no trouble at all. I was able to stay on top of the flight by using the manual controls and this was perhaps the most encouraging part of the entire mission....

In that long plunge back to earth, I was pushed back into the couch with a force of about 11 Gs.... All the way down, as the altimeter spun through mile after mile of descent, I kept grunting out "O.K., O.K., O.K.," just to show them back in the Control Center how I was doing.... All through this period of falling the capsule rolled around very slowly in a counterclockwise direction, spinning at a rate of about 10 degrees per second around its long axis. This was programed to even out the heat and it did not bother me. Neither did the sudden rise in temperature as the friction of the air began to build up outside the capsule. The temperature climbed to 1,230 degrees Fahrenheit on the outer walls. But it never got above 100 degrees in the cabin or above 82 degrees in my suit.... By the time I had fallen to 30,000 feet the capsule had slowed down to about 300 miles per hour. I knew from talking to Deke that my trajectory looked good and that *Freedom 7* was going to land right in the center of the recovery area.... At about 1,000 feet I looked out through the porthole and saw the water coming up towards me. I braced myself in the couch for the impact, but it was not bad at all. It was a little abrupt, but no more severe than the jolt a Navy pilot gets when he is launched off the catapult of a carrier. The spacecraft hit, then flopped over on its side....One porthole was completely under water.... I could not see any water seeping into the capsule, but I could hear all kinds of gurgling sounds around me, so I was not sure whether we were leaking or not. Slowly but steadily the capsule began to right itself. As soon as I knew the radio antenna was out of the water I sent off a message saying that I was fine.

It took the helicopter seven minutes to get me to the carrier. When we approached the ship I could see sailors crowding the deck, applauding and cheering and waving their caps. I felt a real lump in my throat.

—*We Seven, by the Astronauts Themselves,*
by M. Scott Carpenter, et al.

Visitors to the Apollo to the Moon gallery can see Shepard's historic *Freedom 7* Mercury spacecraft. The engineers who went over the capsule after Shepard's flight decided that *Freedom 7* had come through its 15 minute 22 second, 536-mile trip in such good shape that it could be used again.

The next Mercury launch was Gus Grissom's ill-fated, nearly identical, sub-orbital ballistic flight aboard *Liberty Bell 7**

**Freedom 7* had been the seventh Mercury spacecraft built, hence the number 7. However, afterwards, the 7 was retained by the astronauts, who wished to indicate their sense of unity at being the first seven astronauts chosen.

The Freedom 7 *Mercury spacecraft in which, on May 5, 1961, astronaut Alan B. Shepard, became the first American to enter space.*

on July 21, 1961. Grissom's craft had a crack painted on it in honor of its namesake and when, upon landing, its hatch inexplicably blew, flooding the spacecraft and causing it to sink, they lamely joked at the Cape that it was the last time they'd launch a spacecraft with a crack in it. Despite the loss of *Liberty Bell 7*, Grissom's flight was judged so successful that no further Redstone launches were called for. The next mission was John Glenn's three-orbit flight in *Friendship 7*, the spacecraft on exhibit in the Milestones gallery. *Friendship 7* was launched on the morning of February 20, 1962, atop an Atlas launch vehicle whose 360,000-pound thrust accelerated the Mercury spacecraft to an orbital velocity of 17,540 mph in slightly more than 5 minutes. Shepard's and Grissom's suborbital flights had shown that the Mercury spacecraft was a safe vehicle for manned flight; Glenn's *Friendship 7* flight tested the performance of the pilot in a more extended weightless condition and how well the pilot could operate and interact with the various automatic systems in the spacecraft. When an attitude-control rocket malfunctioned during one of the orbits, forcing Glenn to take over manual control of his craft, the advantage of manned space flight was clearly proven. Scott Carpenter in *Aurora 7* duplicated Glenn's three-orbit flight on May 24, 1962. Despite constant problems with faulty instruments, an overheating space suit, and, during preparation for re-entry, misfiring of the rockets, which caused Carpenter to overshoot his target area by some 250 miles, *Aurora 7*'s flight, too, was a success. Wally Schirra in *Sigma 7* was next; his flight was virtually perfect and after six orbits he splashed down only four miles from his recovery ship. The last Mercury flight was Gordon Cooper's *Faith 7* on May 15, 1963. Cooper made 22 orbits and was aloft for 34 hours, 19 minutes, and 49 seconds, an American endurance record, during which he traveled some 583,000 miles.

The Russians, too, had been busy. In August, two months prior to Schirra's flight, the Soviets had launched their most spectacular manned flights. Vostok 3 with Andrian G. Nikolayev was launched August 11, 1962, and the following day Vostok 4 with Pavel R. Popovich was sent up to join him. The two Soviet spacecraft approached to within three miles of each other, but they did not attempt rendezvous. Popovich's 48 orbits and Nikolayev's 64 orbits continued to give the impression that the Soviet space program was more advanced than ours. Not until August 21, 1965, three years after the Vostok 3 and 4 launches, would an American Gemini spacecraft, Gemini 5, carrying astronauts Gordon Cooper and Charles Conrad, Jr., surpass the Soviet endurance record with a flight of 120 orbits lasting eight days. By this time, however, the Soviets had launched two of their Voskhod series spacecraft, which weighed 11,731 pounds, nearly as much as our Apollo spacecraft would weigh five years later. Voskhod 1, launched in October, 1964, had carried three cosmonauts. Voskhod 2, launched March 18, 1965, carried two, Aleksei Leonov and Pavel Belyayev, into a seventeen-orbit mission during which Leonov became the first man to "walk" in space. Difficulties with its automatic navigational system caused the Voskhod 2 to miss its planned landing site in the Ukraine. The spacecraft parachuted to earth far to the frozen north and it took several hours for the spacecraft to be located and nearly a day for a ground party to break through the forest to bring the cosmonauts out on skis. While waiting for rescue, the Soviet crew were forced to remain in their capsule out of fear of the lurking wolves. Ed White's 20-minute "space walk" in Gemini 4 took place not quite three months after Leonov's and was the highlight of Gemini 4's 62-orbit journey on June 3, 1965.

The Gemini 7 spacecraft in the Apollo to the Moon gallery was launched on December 4, 1965, and was followed by Gemini 6 on December 15. Gemini 6, containing astronauts Schirra and Stafford, had been

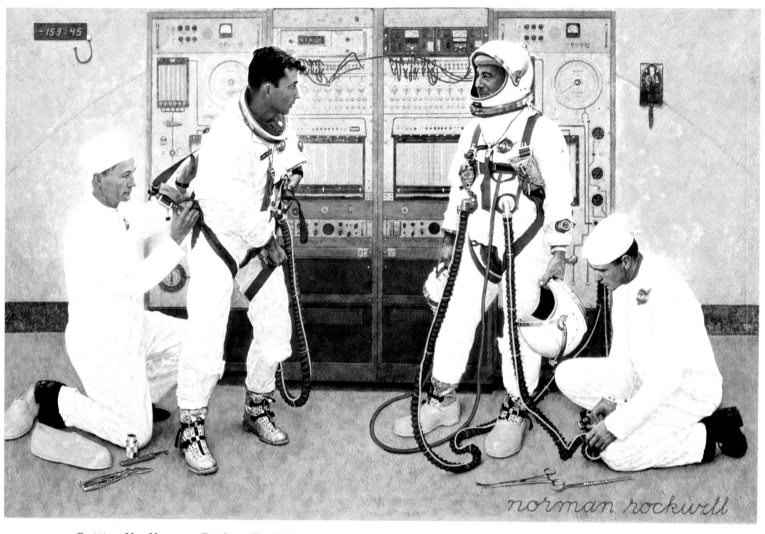

Suiting Up, *Norman Rockwell's 1965 painting of Virgil I. Grissom and John W. Young's Gemini 3 flight captures the intricacies of the preflight preparations.*

scheduled for launch October 25, 1965, to test rendezvous and docking procedures, but it had been delayed when their Agena target vehicle had exploded. Schirra and Stafford had watched the Agena's flawless launch from atop their own Titan II booster and then had begun to busy themselves with their own launch preparations when, six minutes into their target vehicle's flight, all telemetry ceased and the tracking radar at the Cape found itself following not one vehicle but five or six. Gemini 6's attempt at the first space rendezvous docking had to be put off until Gemini 7 could be pressed into service as the "target vehicle."

Gemini 6 was rescheduled for launch on December 12, eight days into Gemini 7's flight,

...and Launch Complex 19 at the Cape again had a Gemini-Titan poised for launch. Wally Schirra and Tom Stafford had no Agena to worry about this time, and all appeared normal during the countdown. In fact, they got engine ignition and an indication of lift-off—then sudden silence. They had about a second to review two scenarios: (1) the engines for some reason had shut down after lift-off, and they were now on the brink of disaster and would either settle back down or topple over, requiring immediate ejection to avoid the ensuing holocaust; (2) the engines had shut down the instant *before* lift-off, in which case they were still firmly bolted to the launch pad and could stay put unless some new danger developed. The design of the hardware spoke for option 1 (supposedly the lift-off signal in the cockpit was foolproof), but the seat of Wally's pants spoke for 2. It felt solid under him. A panicky type might have ejected anyway, and

The cramped Gemini 7 spacecraft in which
Frank Borman and James Lovell, Jr.,
spent two weeks in December, 1965. It was
America's longest manned space flight until
the Skylab missions in 1973.

December, 1965: Gemini 6 and Gemini 7 practiced rendezvous techniques with each other approaching at times as close together as 6 feet. Here Gemini 7 is seen from Gemini 6.

had Wally and Tom done so, certainly no one familiar with the hardware would have blamed them. But supercool Wally kept his head, picked the correct option, and Gemini 6 was saved to fly another day.

    —Carrying the Fire, by Michael Collins

An electrical plug had vibrated loose just after engine ignition and a split second before lift-off, thereby sending a shut-down signal to the engines. It was later found that "a plastic dust cover carelessly left in a fuel line would have blocked the Gemini 6 launch even if an electrical plug had not dropped out of the tail and shut down the Titan II engines."[*] The device, installed at the plant, had not been removed due to "human error." The third launch attempt, on December 15, 1965, was successful, and after chasing Gemini 7 for four orbits, Gemini 6 caught up. The two spacecraft flew in close

---

[*]NASA SP-4006, "Astronautics and Aeronautics, 1965"

formation for five and a half hours, their crews talking back and forth, snapping pictures of one another, and at times approaching as close together as six feet at an altitude of 185 miles. And then, after almost 26 hours in flight, Gemini 6 was recovered while Gemini 7 remained aloft for two more days. On December 18, Frank Borman and James Lovell rotated their Gemini 7 into a retrofire attitude and prepared the electrical circuitry that would fire the retrorockets to bring them back down. These motors had been exposed to the cold vacuum of space for more than two weeks and there was some worry that they might not fire. Mission Control Center was relieved to hear Borman report a successful retrofire, and when the two astronauts were recovered and were seen on television walking confidently across the carrier deck with no apparent serious problems after their record-setting 330-hour endurance flight in space—nearly double the length of time required for a round-trip to the Moon— it now seemed clear that the United States had at last caught up with, if not actually overtaken, the Soviet space effort.

Only five more Gemini flights were planned, and the single major unanswered question that the Gemini program had been designed to resolve was the practicality of a lunar strategy requiring a space rendezvous for its successful completion. An actual docking had yet to take place, and the remaining missions were designed to perfect rendezvous and docking techniques and the sort of Extra-vehicular Activity (EVA) a Moon landing would require. Although Ed White's 22-minute "space walk" on Gemini 4 had been successful, there still did not exist enough practical experience to prove that a man could operate effectively outside of his spacecraft. Gemini 8, launched March 16, 1966, carrying Neil Armstrong and David Scott, completed the first space docking with an Agena target rocket, but when moments later a runaway thruster on the Gemini craft caused the linked vehicles to gyrate uncontrollably, they were forced to undock.

June, 1966: "We have an angry alligator on our hands," radioed Gemini 9's Thomas Stafford as they approached their still nose-shrouded target docking vehicle.

After undocking, the Gemini began to tumble at a rate which built up to 300 degrees per second. Armstrong had to activate the re-entry attitude-control system to bring the spinning Gemini back under control; but once that was done, they had no choice but to return to earth, 60 hours earlier than planned, after spending 10 hours and 42 minutes in space.

Gemini 9, scheduled for launch May 17,

Paul Calle. End of Mercury. *1963. Oil on canvas. On loan from the artist*

1966, had to be delayed when the Atlas booster that was to lift its Agena target vehicle into orbit went out of control, causing the rocket to plunge into the Atlantic. The launch, which was rescheduled for June 1, was delayed once more; but on June 3, Gemini 9 finally thundered into orbit only to discover that the nose shroud of their target vehicle had failed to separate and was instead still attached. Its appearance caused astronaut Stafford to report, "We have an angry alligator on our hands." Cernan's two-hour space walk during this flight was hampered by his exertion, which caused his visor to fog over. Gemini 10, launched July 10, 1966, rendezvoused with two different Agena

vehicles and, after successfully docking with one, astronauts John Young and Michael Collins used its power to propel them into a higher orbit. Collins transmitted a long series of three-digit commands to the Agena to commence its automatic firing sequence, and since they were docked nose-to-nose, the astronauts had the extraordinary experience of watching their own rocket fire up at them:*

---

*Collins' and Young's Gemini 10 was docked on the near end of their Agena, whose engine was mounted on the far end so that they couldn't quite see it. The Agena engine with its 16,000-pound thrust would take them to an altitude of 475 miles, higher than any manned spacecraft had gone before.

At the appointed moment, all I see is a string of snowballs shooting out of the back of the Agena in a widening cone. The unexpected white stream is quite pretty against the black sky. Aw shucks, I think, it's not going to light, when suddenly the whole sky turns orange-white and I am plastered against my shoulder straps. There is no subtlety to this engine, no gentleness in its approach. I am supposed to monitor the status display panel, but I cannot prevent my eyes from wandering past it to the glorious Fourth of July spectacle radiating out from the engine. Out of long habit, however, I check my instruments, and all seems to be going well inside the cockpit. We are swaying mildly back and forth…and as the clock passes through fourteen seconds, I send a command for this raucous engine to cease. At that very instant it has come to the same conclusion, and we are now jerked back into weightlessness and treated to a thirty-second barrage of visual effects even more spectacular than the preliminaries. It is nearly sunset with the sun directly behind us; it clearly illuminates each particle, spark, and fireball coming out of the engine, and there are plenty of them. Some of them are small as fireflies, others large as basketballs; some depart lazily, others zing off at great speed. There is a golden halo encircling the entire Agena that fades very slowly.
—*Carrying the Fire*, by Michael Collins

One of Collins' assigned EVAs was to retrieve a micrometeorite package from an Agena that had been exposed to space for four months:

…Gently, gently I push away from Gemini, hopefully balancing the pressure of my right hand on the open hatch with that of my left hand on the spacecraft itself. As I float out of the cockpit, upward and slightly forward, I note with relief that I am not snagged on anything but am traveling in a straight line with no tendency to pitch or yaw as I go. It's not more than three or four seconds before I collide with my target, the docking adapter on the end of the Agena. A cone-shaped affair with a smooth edge, it is a lousy spot to land because there are no ready handholds, but this is the end where the micrometeorite package is located and, after all, that is what I have come so far to retrieve. I grab the slippery lip of the docking cone with both hands and start working my way around it counterclockwise. It takes about 90 degrees of hand-walking in stiff pressurized gloves to reach the package. As I move I dislodge part of the docking apparatus, an electric discharge ring

which springs loose, dangling from one attaching point. It looks like a thin scythe with a wicked hook, two feet in diameter. I don't know what will happen if I become ensnarled in it…. Best I stay clear of it. By this time, I have reached the package, and now I must stop. Son-of-a-bitch, I am falling off! I have built up too much momentum, and now the inertia in my torso and legs keeps me moving; first my right hand, and then my left, feel the Agena slither away, despite my desperate clutch. As I slowly cartwheel away from the Agena, I see absolutely nothing but black sky for several seconds, and then the Gemini hoves into view. John [Young] has apparently watched all this in silence, but now he croaks, "Where are you, Mike?" "I'm up above. You don't want to sweat it. Only don't go any closer if you can help it. O.K.?" "Yes."
—*Carrying the Fire*, by Michael Collins

Collins did succeed in controlling himself eventually and, with the help of a handheld "maneuvering gun" whose propellant gas would act as a tiny rocket in space, was able to retrieve the micrometeorite package and return to the Gemini.

The final two Gemini flights had astronauts Conrad and Gordon launched in Gemini 11 on September 12, 1966, where they linked up with an orbiting Agena and, using its power, kicked themselves up to a record height of 853 miles. Later, after undocking at 180 miles altitude, the astronauts created some gravity by spinning the two vehicles around each other at the end of a 100-foot rope. Gemini 12, with astronauts Lovell and Aldrin, launched November 11, 1966, concentrated on an extensive EVA, which included simple calisthenics, a space walk, photography, more rendezvous and docking; and the Gemini program was concluded. Borman and Lovell in Gemini 7 had proven that men could remain weightless for fourteen days without suffering any serious consequences; and a lunar landing mission would require only about half as much time.

Gemini 6, 8, 9, 10, 11, and 12 had successfully attempted a variety of rendezvous and docking techniques, proving that a lunar strategy calling for a space rendezvous was practical and that if it could

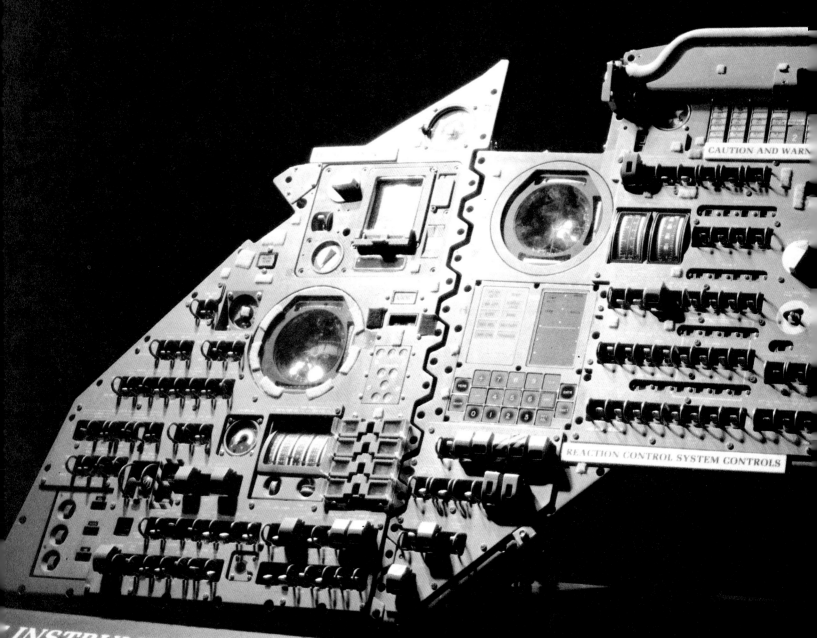

CAUTION AND WARN...

REACTION CONTROL SYSTEM CONTROLS

INSTRUMENT PANEL

...nsole faces the three crew
...Command Module. It
...and meters used to control
... its performance.
...ated sub-systems are
...rols are on the left
...rols are on the

...mand module
...out training.

COMMAND MODULE MA...

SERVICE MODULE PROPULSION SYSTEM CONTROLS

ELECTRICAL POWER CONTROLS

COMMUNICATIONS CONTROLS

N DISPLAY CONSOLE

be done in earth orbit, it could be done around the Moon.

And not the least important by any means was the training and experience gained not only by the astronauts but by the men on the ground; an intricately coordinated, competent testing, planning, and flight control team had been created and had shown its ability to minimize the hazards of sending men on missions a quarter of a million miles from earth and of returning them safely in spite of the problems that arise whenever men deal with complex, unproven machinery in the unknown. It was time to go to the Moon.

By this time tens of thousands of photographs had been taken by American Ranger, Lunar Orbiter, and Surveyor spacecraft and by Russian Luna and Zond vehicles. Both the Americans and Soviets had accomplisehd successful soft landings on the Moon's surface. Lunar Orbiter 1, on August 23, 1966, had returned hundreds of medium-resolution close-ups of potential Apollo landing sites, revealing that the *mare* areas, which appeared so smooth in telescopes, were actually pitted with craters. (Lunar Orbiter 2, launched in November, 1966, had confirmed the puzzling fact, first indicated by Soviet photographs, that there are no large *maria* on the hidden side of the moon.) And then, early in 1967, both the Soviet and the American manned space programs came to a tragic halt.

On January 27, 1967, Mike Collins as senior astronaut present had to attend the Friday staff meeting at Deke Slayton's office. There were very few people around; Slayton,

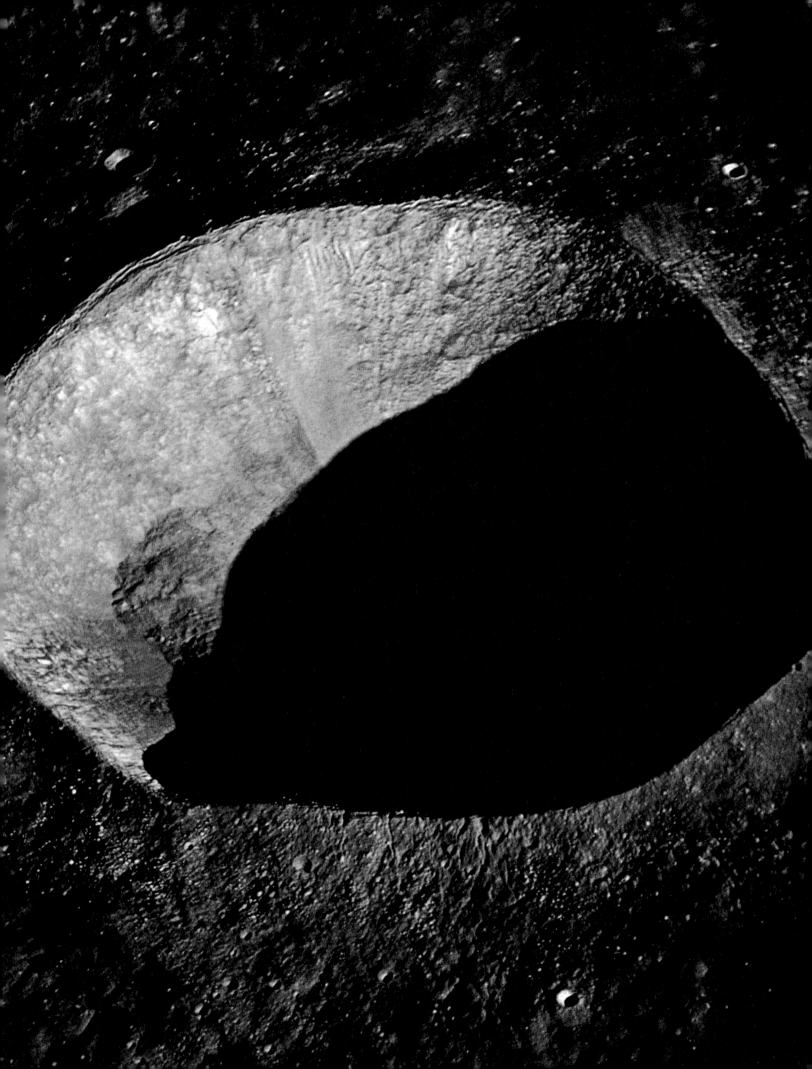

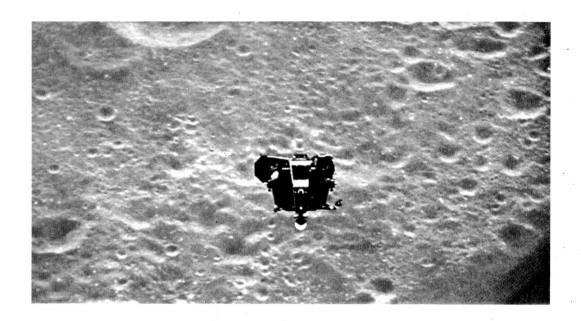

Apollo 10's Lunar Module Snoopy *returns from its trip to within 8.4 miles of the Moon's surface to rendezvous and dock with the Command Module* Charlie Brown.

too, was absent and his assistant Don Gregory was presiding. Collins relates what it was like:

> ...We had just barely gotten started when the red crash phone on Deke's desk rang. Don snatched it up and listened impassively. The rest of us said nothing. Red phones were a part of my life, and when they rang, it was usually a communications test or a warning of an aircraft accident or a plane aloft in trouble. After what seemed a long time, Don finally hung up and said very quietly, "Fire in the spacecraft." That's all he had to say. There was no doubt which spacecraft (012) or who was in it (Grissom-White-Chaffee) or where (Pad 34, Cape Kennedy) or why (a final systems test) or what (death, the quicker the better). All I could think of was, My God, such an obvious thing and yet we hadn't considered it. We worried about engines that wouldn't start or stop; we worried about leaks; we even worried about how a flame front might propagate in weightlessness and how cabin pressure might be reduced to stop fire in space. But right here on the ground, when we should have been most alert, we put three guys inside an untried spacecraft, strapped them into couches, locked two cumbersome hatches behind them, and left them no way of escaping a fire.... As we sat there stunned, the red phone rang again and delivered additional details—rescue crew on the spot but unable to enter because of excessive heat... damage confined to command module alone— no word from the crew or sign of activity from within. Hell no, nor would there ever be—the only question was: How quickly, how quickly?
> —*Carrying the Fire*, by Michael Collins

The deaths of Virgil Grissom, Edward White, and Roger Chaffee brought the United States manned space program to a sudden halt. Not quite three months later, Vladimir Komarov, a veteran Soviet cosmonaut, was killed when his new Soyuz 1 spacecraft, which had been tumbling badly during a flight, was ordered to terminate the mission. During descent, the Soyuz became tangled up in its parachute lines and plunged to earth. The Soviets did not launch another manned spacecraft until October 26, 1968; the Americans, too, had had to extensively redesign their Apollo spacecraft. After two unmanned test flights, astronauts Schirra, Eisele, and Cunningham were launched on October 11, 1968 (twenty-one months after the fatal fire), in Apollo 7 to test the Apollo command module in the relative safety of earth orbit. Their Apollo flight lasted nearly eleven days. The next mission, Apollo 8, would send the Apollo command module and service module to the Moon atop the huge Saturn V rocket, which had not yet been used for a manned flight.

Apollo 8, carrying astronauts Borman, Lovell, and Anders, was launched from Cape Kennedy on December 21, 1968. The giant 364-foot-tall, 6-million-pound Saturn V dwarfed all previous launch vehicles. The main thrust was provided by five F-1 engines clustered together to create 7.6 million pounds of thrust. Visitors to this gallery can get some idea of how huge these engines are by seeing the exhibited F-1 mirrored to create the illusion of all five engines together. The second powered stage contained five J-2 engines, which created a million pounds of thrust; and the third stage contained one J-2 engine atop which was a truncated conical housing that protected and held the lunar module during the flight. Above the third stage was the service module, which held the fuel cells for electrical power in space, tanks, and supporting systems, and a single restartable engine capable of being repeatedly fired in a space environment. This engine propelled and maneuvered the spacecraft once the third stage had been jettisoned. Above the service module was the command module, the crew's quarters during the flight, and the escape tower which would provide their emergency exit in event of trouble on or near the launching pad.

Although Apollo 8's flight might pose fewer unknowns than had Columbus's voyage, as NASA's safety chief Jerry Lederer pointed out three days before the launch, the mission would "involve risks of great magnitude and probably risks that have not been foreseen. Apollo 8 has 5,600,000 parts and one and one half million systems, subsystems, and assemblies. Even if all functioned with 99.9% reliability, we could expect fifty-six hundred defects...." What made Apollo 8's flight different from the six Mercury, ten

As Apollo 11 containing the first men to walk on the Moon swept over the Moon's horizon, the astronauts photographed the awesome majesty of an earthrise from outer space.

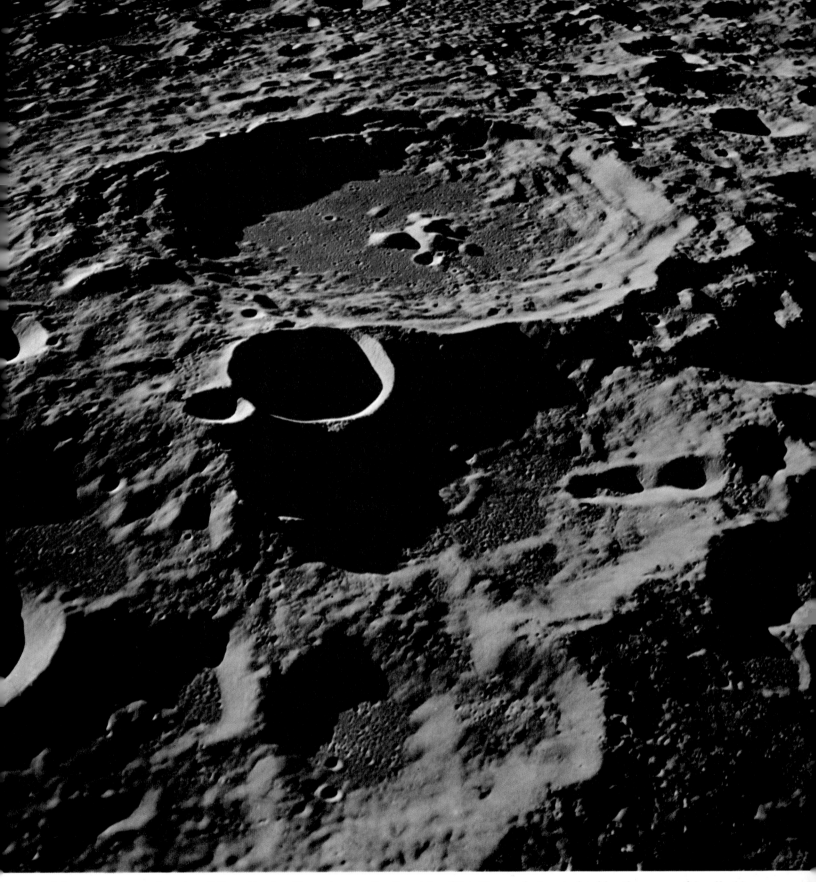

A large un-named crater, fifty miles in diameter, on the far side of the Moon photographed by the crew of Apollo 11.

Overleaf: Interior of the Apollo Lunar Lander from which visitors can watch and hear Apollo 17's landing.

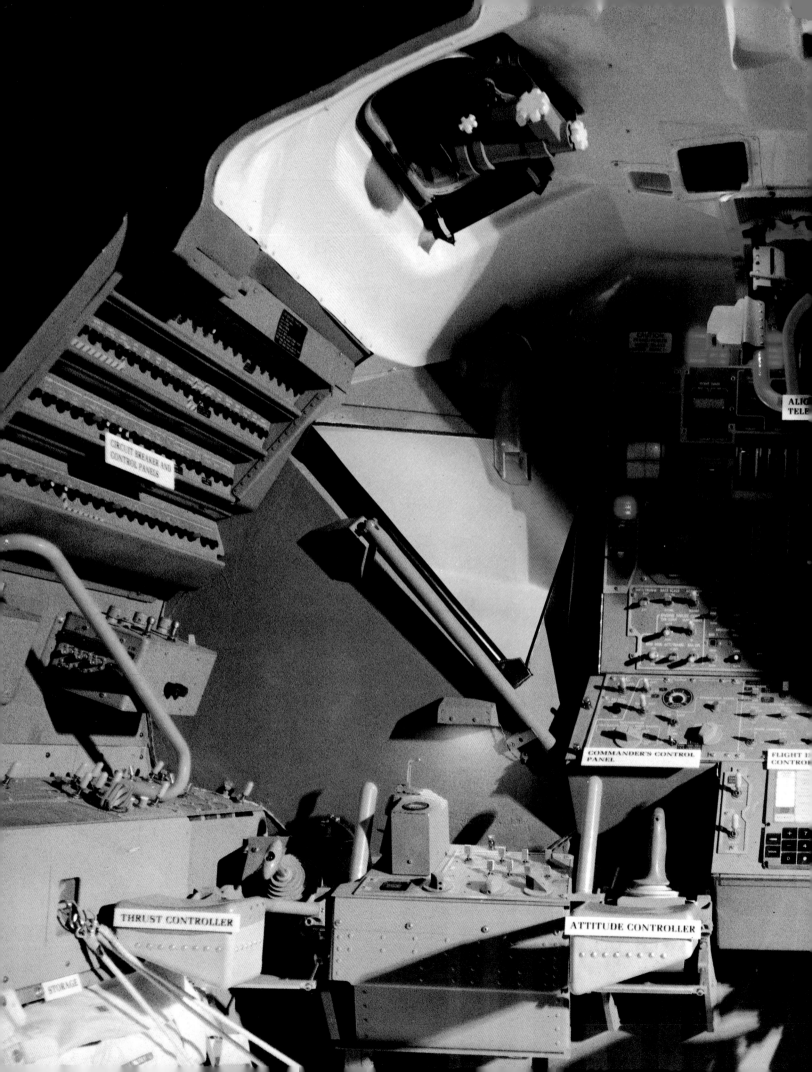

CIRCUIT BREAKER AND
CONTROL PANELS

ALIG
TELE

COMMANDER'S CONTROL
PANEL

FLIGHT I
CONTROL

THRUST CONTROLLER

ATTITUDE CONTROLLER

STORAGE

Lunar Module 2, on exhibit in the Museum's East Gallery, was built for an unmanned earth-orbital test flight. However, the mission of Lunar Module 1 was so successful that it was deemed unnecessary to fly the second craft. While being prepared for exhibition, the craft was outfitted to duplicate the Apollo 11 Lunar Module *Eagle*.

Gemini and one Apollo flight that had
preceded it was that during this mission
for the first time man:

> ...was going to propel himself past escape
> velocity, breaking the clutch of our earth's
> gravitational field and coasting into outer space
> as he had never done before. After TLI [translunar
> injection] there would be three men in the solar
> system who would have to be counted apart from
> all the other billions, three who were in a
> different place, whose motion obeyed different
> rules, and whose habitat had to be considered a
> separate planet. The three could examine the
> earth and the earth could examine them, and
> each would see the other for the first time. This
> the people in Mission Control knew; yet there
> were no immortal words on the wall proclaiming
> the fact, only a thin green line, representing
> Apollo 8 climbing, speeding, vanishing—leaving
> us stranded behind on this planet, awed by the
> fact that we humans had finally had an option to
> stay or to leave—and had chosen to leave.
> —*Carrying the Fire,* by Michael Collins

There were more newspaper reporters at the
Cape for Apollo 8's launch than for any flight
since John Glenn's, and at Mission Control
there was not only the worry at the potential
of mechanical problems, but the necessity
for the absolute accuracy of their navigation,
which required Apollo 8 to miss the Moon by
only eighty miles from a distance of 230,000
miles away. Apollo 8 arrived in orbit around
the Moon on Christmas Eve and the crew
celebrated by taking turns reading from the
King James version of the Bible:

> "In the Beginning God created the Heaven and
> the Earth. And the Earth was without form and
> void. And Darkness was upon the face of the
> Deep....And God saw that it was Good...." And
> from the crew of Apollo 8, we close with good
> night, good luck and a Merry Christmas. And
> God bless all of you, all of you on the good Earth.

During their ten orbits of the Moon, the
astronauts had the opportunity to see sights
never seen before: the first "earth-rise," the
rugged, pockmarked far side of the Moon,

*Neil Armstrong took this photograph of Edwin E.
("Buzz") Aldrin, Jr., saluting the newly planted
American flag on the surface of the Moon as
millions watched on television on Earth.*

So that the Stars and Stripes might "wave" in the airless atmosphere of the
Moon, the flag had to be stiffened with a brace.

and as they circled they took hundreds of photographs, made scientific observations, and shared with millions of people on earth, through live television broadcasts, the incredible scenes they saw. The astronauts found the Moon, "a very whitish gray, like dirty beach sand," and astronaut William Anders thought it "a very dark and unappetizing place." And then it was time for them to restart their SPS engine to come home.

Apollo 9, launched March 3, 1969, was the first manned flight of the lunar module. While Apollo 9 would be a less spectacular flight than the one that had preceded it in that Apollo 9 would never leave earth orbit, it was essential that the practicality of the rendezvous and docking of the Command Service Module (CSM) and the Lunar Module (LM) be tested. The "tissue paper spacecraft," as Jim McDivitt described the thin-skinned LM, was vital to the program and there was no need to fly it all the way to the Moon on its maiden flight. There was, however, the need to make sure everything worked. The Command Service Module had to be separated from the Saturn, turned 180 degrees, then driven back to where the Lunar Module was nestled within its protective sheath, and then docked. Once the CSM and the LM were docked nose to nose, the CSM would pull the LM free of the Saturn. On a lunar flight, this transposition and docking would be done only after the astronauts had been committed to leaving earth orbit and on course for the Moon. Fortunately, Apollo 9 went smoothly. The CSM pulled the LM free, and then they undocked from each other to perform a series of maneuvers which took them as far as 100 miles apart. They then duplicated as exactly as possible the sort of maneuvers and techniques required for a Lunar Module crew ascending from the Moon's surface to link back up with their Command Service Module.

Since Apollo 8's lunar flight had been successful and Apollo 9's had shown that the LM and CSM could transpose, dock, and rendezvous successfully, and since Apollo 10

was scheduled to be launched in just two more months, in May, why shouldn't Apollo 10's mission (which called for Tom Stafford and Gene Cernan to separate their LM from the CSM piloted by John Young and to descend to 50,000 feet above the lunar surface) attempt a lunar landing? There were many reasons, some having to do with the Moon being an entirely different environment in which to attempt a rendezvous, the lighting conditions, the orbital velocities, the ground tracking capabilities being different; an added complication was that the gravitational pull of the Moon was not evenly distributed and not enough information had been gained about where the concentrations of heavy-gravity spots were located to permit the tracking people with their computers to know exactly when and how they might affect an orbiting LM or CSM. The final argument was that Stafford's LM was some pounds overweight—which meant little in orbit, but which might be of immense significance when the time came to lift the LM off the surface of the Moon.

Apollo 10, launched on May 18, 1969, was the only full "dress rehearsal" for man's landing on the Moon. Astronauts Stafford and Cernan took their LM, *Snoopy*, down to 8.4 miles above the lunar surface to check out the Apollo 11 landing site in the Sea of Tranquility. After two passes and radioing back the description of the site's surface being "pretty smooth—like wet clay," they fired their ascent engine and rendezvoused with astronaut Young in the CSM, *Charlie Brown*. There was nothing left to do but to land men on the Moon.

On the morning of July 16, 1969, while astronauts Neil Armstrong, Michael Collins, and Buzz Aldrin were going through their final checklists prior to launch, Hermann Oberth was at the Cape to watch them go. He was seventy-five years old now, bent, white-haired, and the only one of the three great pioneers still alive. Tsiolkovsky had died in 1935, Goddard ten years later. Charles Lindbergh was there, too, along with T. Claude Ryan, who had built the *Spirit of St. Louis.* Everybody "who was anybody" or "had

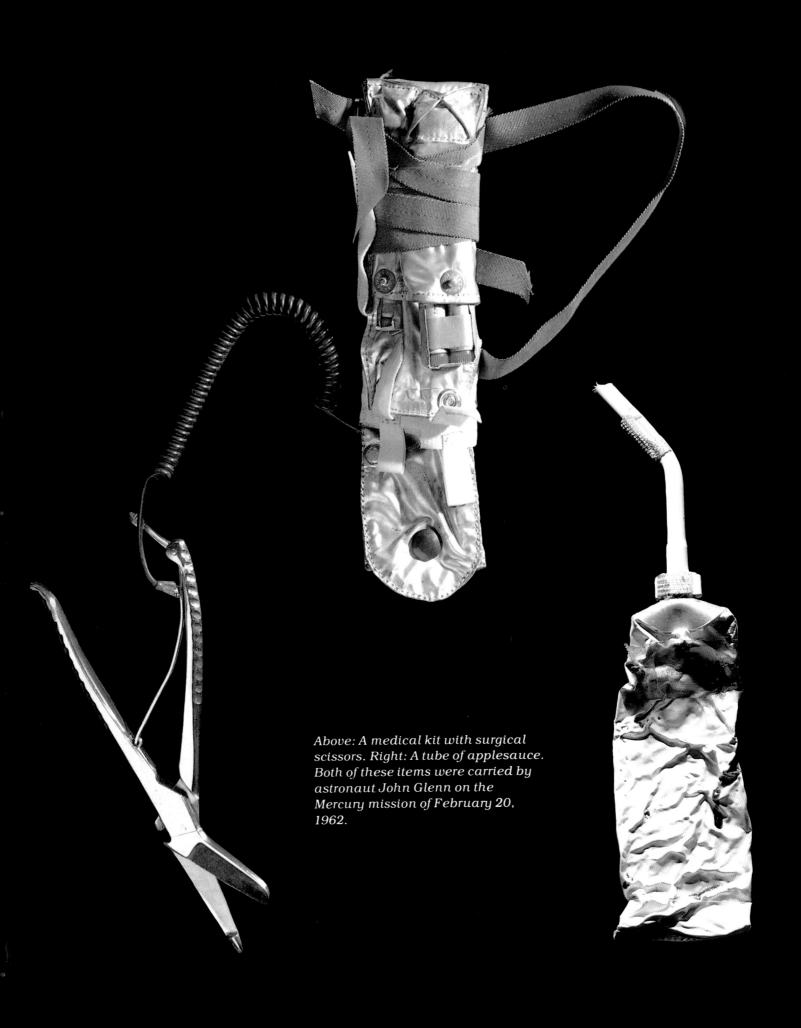

Above: A medical kit with surgical scissors. Right: A tube of applesauce. Both of these items were carried by astronaut John Glenn on the Mercury mission of February 20, 1962.

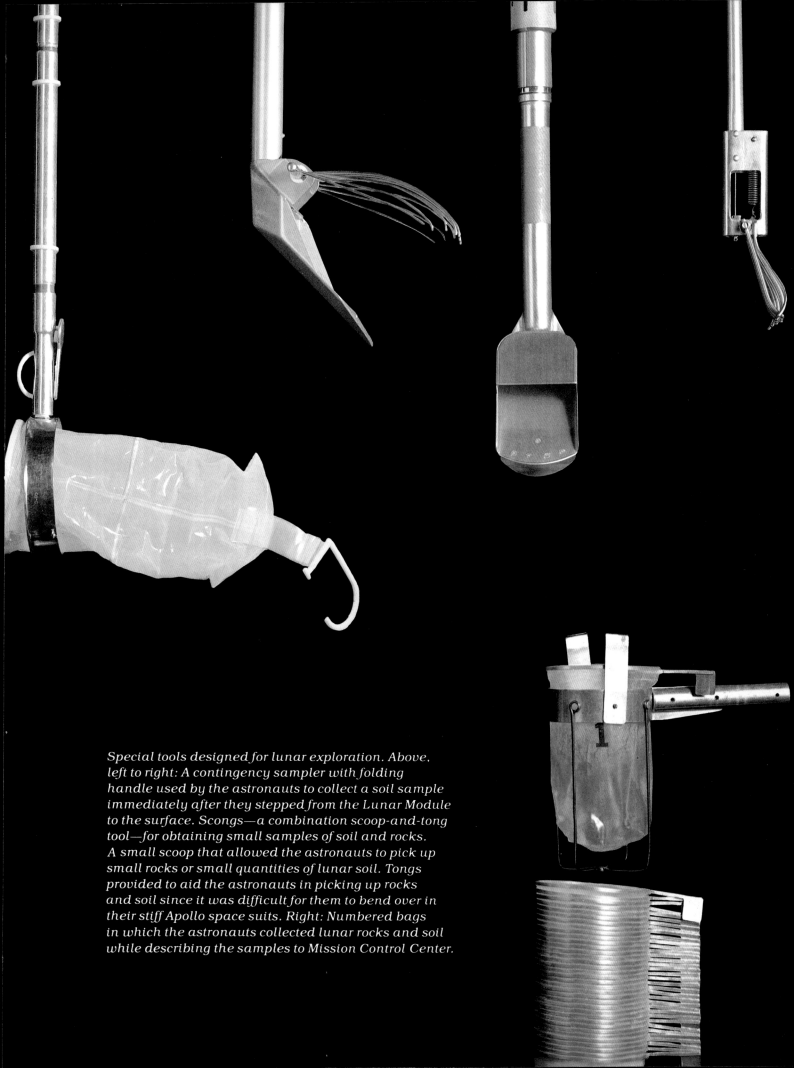

Special tools designed for lunar exploration. Above, left to right: A contingency sampler with folding handle used by the astronauts to collect a soil sample immediately after they stepped from the Lunar Module to the surface. Scongs—a combination scoop-and-tong tool—for obtaining small samples of soil and rocks. A small scoop that allowed the astronauts to pick up small rocks or small quantities of lunar soil. Tongs provided to aid the astronauts in picking up rocks and soil since it was difficult for them to bend over in their stiff Apollo space suits. Right: Numbered bags in which the astronauts collected lunar rocks and soil while describing the samples to Mission Control Center.

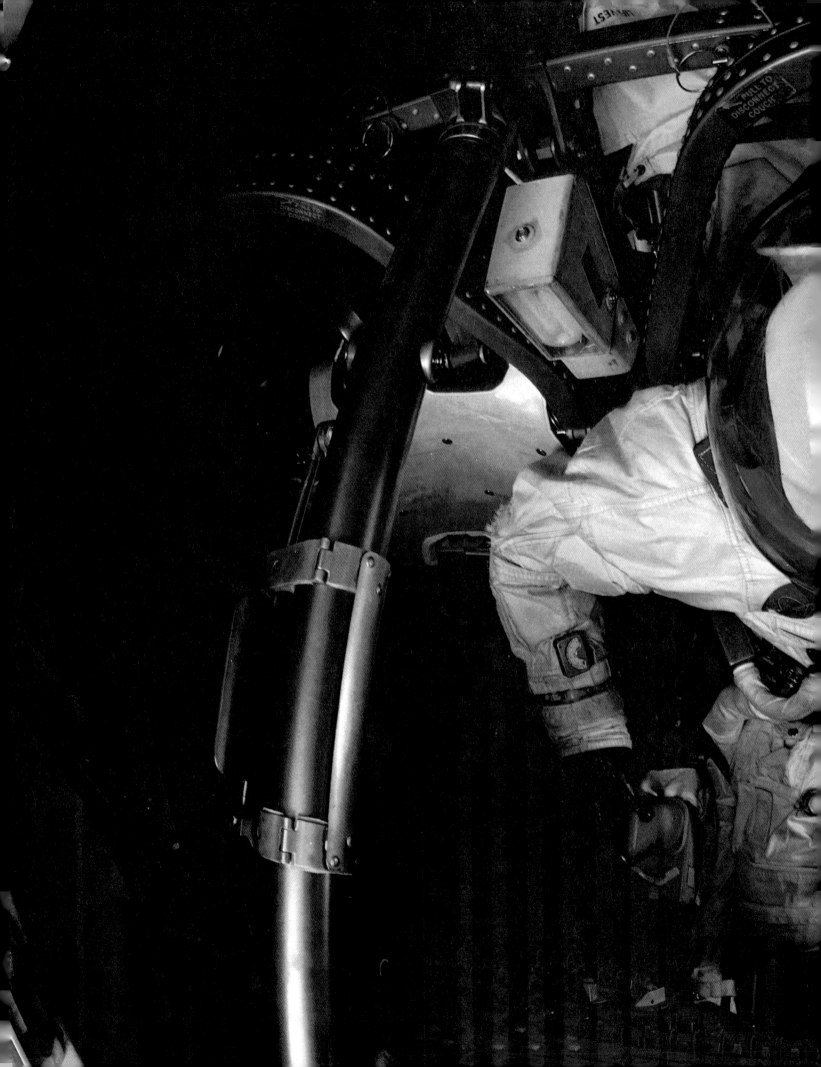

One of the vesicular basalt rocks formed by lunar vulcanism 3.7 billion years ago that was collected on the Moon and returned to this planet by astronauts during the six lunar landings of the Apollo program.

Preceding page: Interior of the Apollo 11 Command Module.

Chesley Bonestell. **End of the World.** *Oil on panel, 16 1/4 x 28 1/4". On loan from Alfred L. Weisbrich*

been anybody in the space program" was at the Cape to watch the launching of Apollo 11.

T minus sixty seconds and counting, Fifty-five seconds and counting. Neil Armstrong just reported back. It's been a real smooth countdown. We have passed the fifty-second mark. Our transfer is complete on internal power with the launch vehicle at this time. Forty seconds away...all the second stage tanks are now pressurized. Thirty-five seconds and counting. We are still go with Apollo 11. Thirty seconds and counting. Astronauts reported, feel good. T minus twenty-five seconds, guidance is internal. Twelve, eleven, ten, nine, ignition sequence starts. Six, five, four, three, two, one, zero, all engines running. LIFTOFF! We have a liftoff, thirty-two minutes past the hour. Liftoff on Apollo 11. Tower cleared.

—*First on the Moon*, by Neil Armstrong, Michael Collins, Edwin E. Aldrin, Jr., with Gene Farmer and Dora Jane Hamblin

Michael Collins thought the first fifteen seconds "quite a rough ride":

...I suppose Saturns are like people in a way—no two of them are exactly the same....It was very busy. It was steering like crazy. It was like a woman driving her car down a very narrow alleyway. She can't decide whether she's too far to the left or too far to the right, but she knows she's one or the other. And she keeps jerking the wheel back and forth. Think about a nervous, very nervous lady. Not a drunk lady. The drunk lady would probably be more relaxed and do a much better job. So there we were just very busy, steering. It was all very jerky and I was glad when they called "Tower clear" because it was nice to know there was no structure around when this thing was going through its little hiccups and jerks.

> —*First on the Moon*, by Neil Armstrong,
> Michael Collins, Edwin E. Aldrin, Jr.,
> with Gene Farmer and Dora Jane Hamblin

After a four-day voyage, the Lunar Module *Eagle* and the Command Service Module *Columbia* (named, in part, after the *Columbiad*, the cannon that fired a manned projectile to the Moon in Jules Verne's 1865 classic, *From the Earth to the Moon*) entered lunar orbit, averaging sixty miles above its surface so that they had a "noticeable sensation of speed." However, Collins noted:

It's not quite as exhilarating a feeling as orbiting the earth, but it's close. In addition, it has an exotic, bizarre quality due entirely to the nature of the surface below. The earth from orbit is a delight—alive, inviting, enchanting—offering visual variety and an emotional feeling of belonging "down there." Not so with this withered, sun-seared peach pit out my window. There is no comfort to it; it is too stark and barren; its invitation is monotonous and meant for geologists only.

> —*Carrying the Fire*, by Michael Collins

The day before, as they had swung their spacecraft around to view the approaching Moon, Collins had sensed the Moon's hostile forbiddingness: "This cool, magnificent sphere hangs there ominously," he later wrote, "a formidable presence without sound or motion, issuing us no invitation to invade its domain." Neil Armstrong had commented then that it was "a view worth the price of the trip." Collins had added, "And somewhat scary too, although no one says that." Now it is time to separate the *Eagle* from *Columbia*. And while *Columbia* with Collins

orbits overhead, the *Eagle* descends gradually to inspect its landing site more closely. On its second pass, a little more than 102 hours and 45 minutes after leaving Cape Kennedy, the following dialogue takes place. LMP = Lunar Module (*Eagle*) Pilot, Buzz Aldrin; CDR = Commander, Neil Armstrong; CMP = Command Module (*Columbia*) Pilot, Michael Collins; CC = Capsule Communicator, at Houston. 04 06 44 45 is the elapsed time of the flight: 4th day, 6th hour, 44th minute, 45th second.

04 06 44 45	LMP	100 feet, 3½ down, 9 forward. Five percent.
04 06 44 54	LMP	Okay. 75 feet, There's looking good. Down a half. 6 forward.
04 06 45 02	CC	60 seconds
04 06 45 04	LMP	Lights on…
04 06 45 08	LMP	Down 2½. Forward…Forward …Good.
04 06 45 17	LMP	40 feet, down 2½. Kicking up some dust.
04 06 45 21	LMP	30 feet, 2½ down. Faint shadow.
04 06 45 25	LMP	4 forward…4 forward. Drifting to the right a little. Okay. Down a half.
04 06 45 31	CC	30 seconds.
04 06 45 32	CDR	Forward drift?
04 06 45 33	LMP	Yes.
04 06 45 34	LMP	Okay.
04 06 45 40	LMP	CONTACT LIGHT
04 06 45 43	LMP	Okay. ENGINE STOP.
04 06 45 45	LMP	ACA—out of DETENT.
04 06 45 46	CDR	Out of DETENT.
04 06 45 47	LMP	MODE CONTROL—both AUTO. DESCENT ENGINE COMMAND OVERRIDE—OFF. ENGINE ARM—OFF.

The Apollo 11 Command Module Columbia, charred and flaked
from its fiery re-entry, being hoisted onto the deck of the
aircraft carrier Hornet 950 miles southwest of Hawaii. The
Columbia's flotation balloons are still attached.

Overleaf: Interior of the Apollo Command Module.

04 06 45 52	LMP	413 is in.
04 06 45 57	CC	We copy you down, Eagle.
04 06 45 59	CDR	Houston, Tranquility Base here.
04 06 46 04	CDR	THE EAGLE HAS LANDED.
04 06 46 04	CC	Roger, Tranquility. We copy you on the ground. You got a bunch of guys about to turn blue. We're breathing again. Thanks a lot.
04 06 46 16	CDR	Thank you.

Astronauts Armstrong and Aldrin were busy for a while, then Armstrong called Houston again:

04 06 55 16	CDR	Hey, Houston, that may have seemed like a very long final phase. The auto targeting was taking us right into a football-field-sized crater with a large number of big boulders and rocks for about...one or two crater diameters around it, and it required a...in P66 and flying manually over the rockfield to find a reasonably good area.
04 06 55 49	CC	Roger. We copy. It was beautiful from here, Tranquility. Over.
04 06 56 02	LMP	We'll get to the details of what's around here, but it looks like a collection of just about every variety of shape, angularity, granularity, about every variety of rock you could find. The colors—well, it varies pretty much depending on how you're looking relative to the zero-phase point. There doesn't appear to be too much of a general color at all. However, it looks as though some of the rocks and boulders, of which there are quite a few in the near area, it looks as though they're going to have some interesting colors to them. Over.

The relief and exhilaration expressed by Mission Control over *Eagle's* safe landing was echoed all over the world, but, almost immediatcly, tension again built in anticipation of Armstrong and Aldrin's first steps on the Moon. After six and a half hours of preparation and as an estimated 600 million people throughout the world clustered around television sets, the hatch opened and slowly, very carefully Neil Armstrong began to climb out. The first thing anyone saw was Armstrong's leg:

> HOUSTON: Okay, Neil, we can see you coming down the ladder now.
> ARMSTRONG: Okay, I just checked—getting back up to that first step. Buzz, it's not even collapsed too far, but it's adequate to get back up...It takes a pretty good little jump...I'm at the foot of the ladder. The LM footpads are only depressed in the surface about one or two inches. Although the surface appears to be very, very fine-grained, as you get close to it. It's almost like a powder. Now and then, it's very fine...I'm going to step off the LM now...[*I had thought about what I was going to say, largely because so many people had asked me to think about it. I thought about that a little on the way to the Moon, and it wasn't really decided until after we got onto the lunar surface. I guess I hadn't actually decided what I wanted to say until just before we went out...*] THAT'S ONE SMALL STEP FOR A MAN, ONE GIANT LEAP FOR MANKIND. *

It was 9:56 PM in Houston, July 20, 1969. Man was standing on the Moon. President Kennedy's goal of landing a man on the Moon before the decade was out had been achieved. It had required eight years, an expenditure of $25 billion dollars, and the greatest technological mobilization the world has known. Visitors to the Apollo to the Moon gallery must remind themselves that when, on January 31, 1958, the United States placed its first satellite, the 31-pound *Explorer*, into orbit it was

---

*When Apollo 12 flight commander Charles "Pete" Conrad stepped on the moon on November 19, 1969, thereby becoming the third man to do so, he jubilantly paraphrased Armstrong, saying, "Whoopee, man, that may have been a small step for Neil, but that's a long one for me."

Enveloped in a cloud of blue vapor from his own Portable Life Support System, astronaut Alan L. Bean of Apollo 12 strides across the surface of the Moon.

The first motor vehicle on the Moon was Apollo 15's Lunar Roving Vehicle, which was driven 17.3 miles at a top speed of 7-8 miles per hour. LRV's were also used on Apollo missions 16 and 17 and made it possible for the astronauts to carry heavy, bulky equipment and scientific instruments to locations distant from their Lunar Modules.

considered an outstanding technological achievement. And yet within eleven years the Saturn V rocket, which was capable of orbiting 140 *tons*, would carry men to the Moon—and back. In 1958, to put one pound in orbit cost half a million dollars; by 1968 the Saturn was orbiting a pound for $500. Nevertheless, as Arthur C. Clarke pointed out, "It is impossible to tolerate indefinitely a situation in which a gigantic, complex vehicle like a Saturn V is used for a single mission, and destroys itself during the flight. The Cunard Line would not stay in business for long if the *Queen Elizabeth* carried three passengers—and sank after her maiden voyage."

The Apollo Program ended in December, 1972, after twelve astronauts* had walked on and explored the Moon and brought back 843 pounds of rocks. These rocks are made up of the same chemicals as earth rocks; but the proportions are different. Moon rocks contain more calcium, aluminum, and titanium than earth rocks and more rare elements like hafnium and zirconium. Other elements with low melting points, such as potassium and sodium, are more scarce in Moon rocks. The chemical composition of the Moon is different in different places: the light-colored highlands are rich in calcium and aluminum; the dark-colored *maria* contain less of those elements and more titanium, iron, and magnesium.

The inside of the Moon is not uniform; it is divided into layers. There is an outer crust probably composed of calcium and aluminum-rich rocks to a depth of about 37 miles. Beneath this crust is the mantle, a thick layer of denser rocks extending down to more than 500 miles. The deep

interior is still unknown. The Moon does not have a magnetic field like the Earth's and yet magnetism has been discovered in many of the older Moon rocks that were brought back. Perhaps the Moon had an ancient magnetic field which disappeared after the old rocks were formed.

If, after viewing Alan Shepard's *Freedom 7* Mercury spacecraft, Frank Borman's and James Lovell, Jr.'s Gemini 7, the Lunar Roving Vehicle (three of these vehicles, used by the crews of Apollo 15, 16, and 17 are still on the Moon; the Museum's specimen was used in tests), the huge Saturn F-1 engine, the tools used by the astronauts, the Apollo Command Module from Skylab 4 (which ferried astronauts Gibson, Carr, and Pogue up to the Skylab for the last and longest, at 84 days, mission), and the various rocks and artifacts from the Moon, the visitor to the gallery is cynical enough to wonder whether all those billions of dollars spent were worth it, it would be nice for him to consider this editorial from the London *Economist* two days after Apollo 11 had safely returned to earth:

> And as the excitement dies and familiarity sets in, the voices that say the money could be better spent on ending wars and poverty on earth must gain converts.
> But this argument overlooks the factor in human make-up that sets us apart from the apes. When man first became a tool-maker, he ceased to be a monkey. The human race's way of sublimating its highest aspirations has been to build the greatest and grandest artifact that the technology of the time can achieve. Through the pyramids, the parthenons and the temples, built as they were on blood and bones, to the be-spired cathedrals conceived and constructed in ages of great poverty, the line runs unbroken to the launch pad of Apollo 11. Oddly—or perhaps not so oddly—the churchmen with their unstinting praise of the astronauts have recognized this where the liberally educated rationalists with their bored carping, and their ill-bred little jokes, have not. Spiralling to the planets expresses something in human nature that relieving poverty, however a noble cause that is, does not. And to the planets, sooner rather than later, man is now certain to go.

---

*The crews of the Moon landing missions were as follows: Apollo 11—Armstrong, Collins, Aldrin; Apollo 12—Conrad, Gordon, Bean; Apollo 14—Shepard, Roosa, Mitchell; Apollo 15—Scott, Worden, Irwin; Apollo 16—Young, Mattingly, Duke; Apollo 17—Cernan, Evans, Schmitt. (In each case, the second astronaut listed was the Command Module pilot, who did not walk on the Moon.)

Skylab

The Space Hall is the third of the three huge exhibit halls facing the Mall (the other two being Milestones of Flight and the Hall of Air Transportation), and among its guided missiles, space launch vehicles, Skylab, the Apollo-Soyuz test project, Space Shuttle, and space missions of the future—exhibits which span the developments made in space flight from World War II through a hypothetical lunar base—are some of the largest artifacts in the Museum.

After World War II ended in 1945, Germany was between five and seven years ahead of all the other countries in rocket development—although it had not always been that way. When Dr. Wernher von Braun examined American rocket pioneer Robert H. Goddard's patents after the war, he had said, "Goddard was ahead of us all." Von Braun meant Goddard had been ahead until 1936, though even by then Colonel Walter Dornberger and Von Braun's team of engineers working for the German Army Weapons Department had already begun development of an engine for the A-4, a large rocket-propelled projectile, later designated the V-2. But while Robert Goddard and his crew of welders, instrument makers, and machinists (a team which never numbered more than seven persons, including Goddard and his wife Esther, who served as official photographer and volunteer fireman) conducted their liquid-propelled rocket experiments—a labor made possible by a $50,000 two-year Guggenheim grant—the Von Braun organization, numbering some 10,000, their research backed by millions of *Deutschmarks* funded by the German army and air force, worked at expressly constructed test facilities at Peenemünde, Germany. As Frederick C. Durant III, NASM's Assistant Director of Astronautics and one of the foremost authorities on Robert H. Goddard, explains, "That is why the Germans were literally years ahead of the Allies in 1945 in all areas of rocket and missile development. The V-2 represented

a quantum jump, a new plateau of technological capability in rocket and missile propulsion, guidance, aerodynamics, instrumentation, etc."

Components for nearly 100 captured V-2s were shipped to the White Sands Proving Grounds in New Mexico after the war and were used for training American personnel in the handling and launch operations of large rockets, as well as for lofting high-altitude, scientific data-gathering instrumentation. In 1946, sixteen V-2 flights were made, four of them to altitudes over 100 miles. It was to be months before the first American Aerobee and years before the first Viking sounding rockets were flown, and still longer before such altitudes were reached.

Whereas in the Satellite and Apollo to the Moon galleries the emphasis is primarily on payloads, here in the Space Hall's guided missile and space launch vehicle exhibit the focus is on the rockets that placed those payloads where they were supposed to go. The 46-foot-tall V-2, the world's first long-range ballistic missile, was seminal to all the large post-war launch vehicles designed to deliver intercontinental ballistic missile warheads and to place satellites in orbit, which led to men landing on the Moon and which send unmanned spacecraft to the outer planets. (Suspended above the V-2 are a number of rare German ground-to-air, air-to-air, and ground-to-ground missiles, among them the infamous V-1, known to wartime Londoners as the "Buzz Bomb.") The modern strategic missile systems that form the backbone of our national defense also made possible our entry into space. Nowhere is this lineage more evident than with the Jupiter-C rocket that stands in the pit near the V-2. The Jupiter-C, which launched America's first satellite, Explorer 1, on January 31, 1958, is nothing more than a modified Redstone Ballistic Missile, a 500-mile-range rocket developed for the United States Army in the early 1950s by Dr. Wernher von Braun and his team,

many of whom had worked on the V-2.

The 68-foot-tall Jupiter-C shares the pit with a 70.8-foot-tall Vanguard (which launched our second satellite), a 73.8-foot NASA Scout (the only all-solid-propellant satellite launch vehicle), and a 60.4-foot United States Air Force Minuteman 3, a contemporary ICBM and one of our major strategic defense missiles. A Poseidon C-3, the two-stage United States Navy Fleet Ballistic Missile that is designed to be launched underwater from nuclear submarines, is displayed horizontally nearby.

It may help the Museum visitor to grasp the enormous size of an actual Saturn V launch vehicle by looking at the 48-foot-long, 80,000-pound Skylab Orbital Workshop and its 17-foot-long, 45,000-pound Multiple Docking Adapter and Airlock Module that dominate the Space Hall. The entire Skylab cluster consisted of four parts: the Orbital Workshop (OWS), the Airlock Module (AM), the Apollo Telescope Mount (ATM), and the Multiple Docking Adapter (MDA). In orbit the Skylab cluster was 118.1 feet long and weighed 199,750 pounds. The Saturn V rocket that launched these huge devices into orbit stood 364 feet tall—as high as a 36-story building, three-fifths the height of the Washington Monument, and more than half as long as the National Air and Space Museum itself.

When the scheduled number of lunar landings was reduced, the Saturn V and IB launch vehicles no longer needed for Apollo were utilized by Skylab.

Skylab was a space station* launched into

---

*It can be argued that Skylab was not, strictly speaking, a "space station," which is usually defined as a structure that can be indefinitely resupplied with consumable items. Skylab could be resupplied with some items, but there were no fittings to enable the station to be resupplied with nitrogen, oxygen, or water, and, after its effective life, it would necessarily have to be abandoned.

Earth orbit on May 14, 1973, and manned on three different occasions by three-man Skylab astronaut teams. The first Skylab crew, consisting of Charles Conrad, Jr., Joseph P. Kerwin, and Paul J. Weitz, were in space from May 25 through June 22, 1973, a period of 28 days. The second crew, Alan L. Bean, Owen K. Garriott, and Jack R. Lousma, was launched a month later, on July 28 and spent 59 days, until September 25th, aboard the space station. The third crew, Gerald P. Carr, Edward G. Gibson, and William R. Pogue, arrived on November 16, 1973:

> On that day, the space station—gold, white, and silver—was hard to make out against the swirling white clouds of the earth 269 miles below. Skylab resembled a huge, squat helicopter with a tower overhead surmounted by what looked like a big four-bladed rotor, but which was in fact an array of solar panels for generating electricity. It was somewhat battered now. After six months in space, the white paint had browned slightly, and some of the gold had baked and blackened. It was minus one pair of stubby, winglike solar panels that had broken off shortly after it was launched from Cape Kennedy [on May 14, 1973]; in the mishap, insulation protecting it from the sun had been shredded from its surface. The first crew [which had arrived twelve days later, on May 26, 1973] had erected a protected parasol over the space station; and the second crew [which had arrived on July 28] had spread a huge awning over that. Consequently, with its awning and its parasol, its pinwheel of solar panels overhead and its single remaining wing, Skylab looked less now like a space station than like Uncle Wiggily's airship.
>
> —*A House in Space,* by Henry S.F. Cooper, Jr.

In some ways Skylab was a far more ambitious and critically important program than Apollo to the Moon despite the "poor cousin" impression one might gather from its having been knocked together out of surplus Apollo parts. But if Skylab was not as dramatic a program as sending men to the Moon, it had a wholly different character and intent. Just as Gemini 7's fourteen-day flight had proven men could endure the prolonged weightless state required by a trip to the Moon and back, the eighty-four-day mission of Skylab's third crew proved that men might physically endure a flight to Mars. And, even though during the Skylab program the astronauts conducted various scientific experiments and performed a variety of tasks with an array of sophisticated equipment, the major scientific experiment—if not in fact the chief purpose of the Skylab program—was to see what happened to the astronauts themselves.

> From the standpoint of time spent in space, as well as from the standpoint of the large size of the space station, both of which imposed special sets of circumstances, Skylab extended man's experience in a new way. The difference between it and earlier missions was between going on a quick trip through space in a vehicle the size of a car,* and moving there to stay a while in a house with all its rooms and corridors. The Skylab astronauts were the first to live in weightlessness. Like many long visits, the ones aboard Skylab were almost like a state of mind. It was not suspenseful, like the expeditions to the moon, but a steady, continuous experience, like life anywhere.
>
> On a normal day during the third mission, the three astronauts were awakened by a buzzer at six o'clock in the morning, Central Standard Time, the time at the Johnson Space Center outside Houston, from which the flight was controlled. They felt refreshed; they logged much more sleep than the Apollo astronauts, who had been under more strain and had not had their own individual bedrooms....Before they could get out of their beds, which were sort of sleeping bags hung vertically against the walls of their bedrooms, they had to unzip a light cloth that had kept them from floating off during the night. Then they soared upward out of bed as if by magic—as though they were genii escaping from bottles. They moved about without using their feet; and even if they made their feet go through the motions of walking, and then stopped these motions, they kept right on going until they hit something. If they thrust out an arm in one

---

*Michael Collins said of the Gemini, "It's so *damned* small, smaller than the front seat of a Volkswagen, with a large console between the pilots, sort of like having a color TV set in a VW separating two adults.... The cockpit was tiny, the two windows were tiny, the pressure suits were big and bulky, and there were a million items of loose equipment which constantly had to be stowed and restowed." [from *Carrying the Fire*]

> direction, they moved back in the other. They could not have experienced these phenomena as readily in the smaller craft used by earlier astronauts; by its size, Skylab added a dimension to weightlessness. The astronauts, and everything they handled, moved as though they were underwater, in a sort of dreamlike, disembodied way—or as though they were in a magical place. They *were*, of course, if by magic is meant a suspension of natural laws familiar on earth. For two billion years, life on this planet has been conditioned by those laws, and all evolution has been determined by them. In gravity, where everything has weight, skeletons are needed for rigidity and leverage, muscles are needed for any sustained motion, and a circulatory system is required to pump blood against gravity. Arms, legs, fins, and cilia have all been developed for locomotion in gravity. Now, in weightlessness, all the effects of gravity vanished, and with them many of the reasons men are the way they are.
>
> Before Skylab, nobody had known much about the long-term effects of weightlessness on man, and it was the purpose of the project to find out what they are—together with assessing what sort of useful work man might do in space, and how he might comfortably live in his new environment.
>
> —*A House in Space*, by Henry S.F. Cooper, Jr.

Several disturbing symptoms had arisen in astronauts who had spent any extended period of time weightless in space. When Frank Borman and Jim Lovell returned from their two-week orbital flight aboard Gemini 7, flight surgeons detected a loss of muscle tissue (which led to diminished physical strength), a loss of calcium from their bones (diminished strength), and a sizable loss in the amount of bodily fluids, including blood which now contained fewer red cells. The astronauts' cardiovascular systems (heart and blood vessels) had weakened, and their body fluids had been redistributed to their upper from their lower parts. There was no way for the doctors to know whether these adverse changes in the astronauts' bodies were indications of unalterable courses— that the longer an astronaut was weightless, the worse his condition became—or whether these adverse changes progressed to a certain point and then ceased, or whether the body eventually compensated for the lack of gravity and

Skylab's Multiple Docking Adapter and Airlock Module.

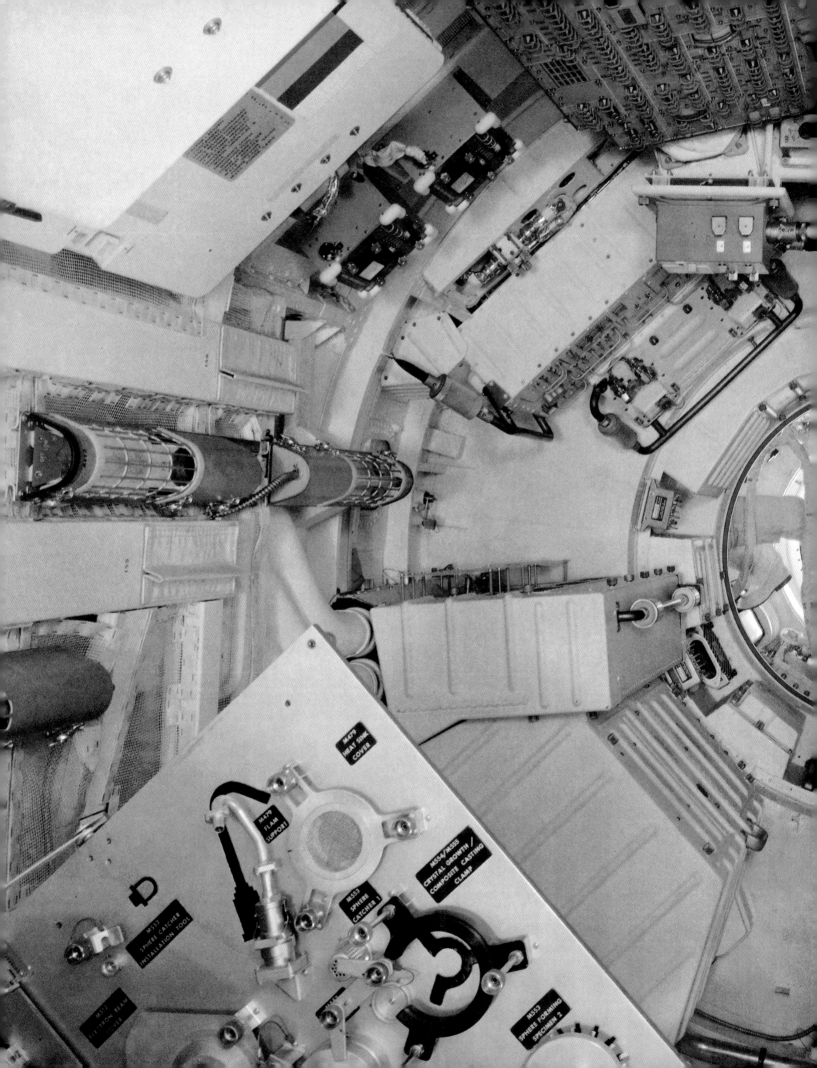

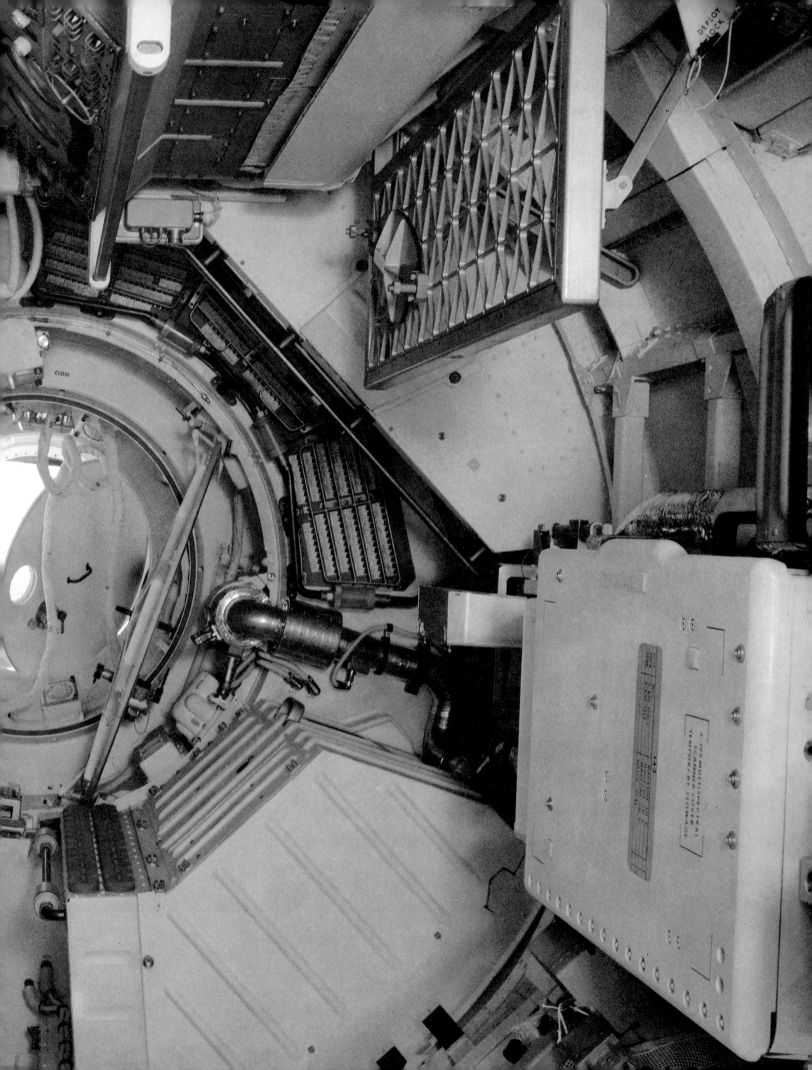

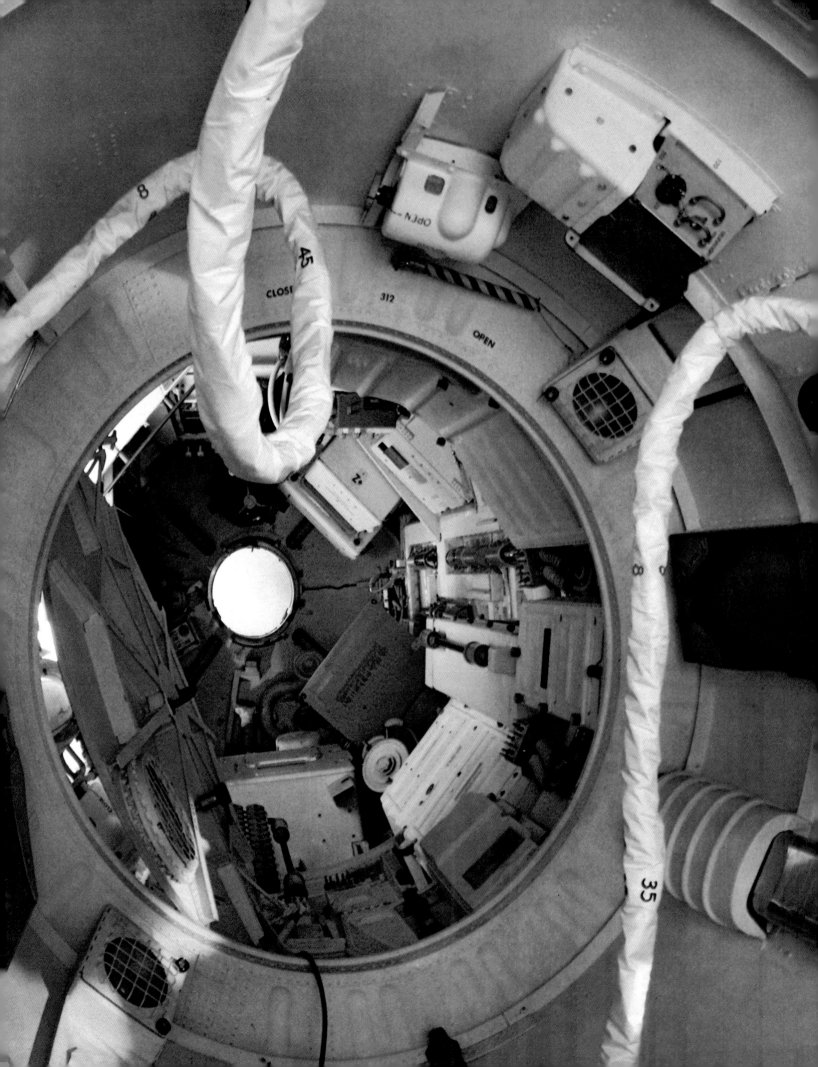

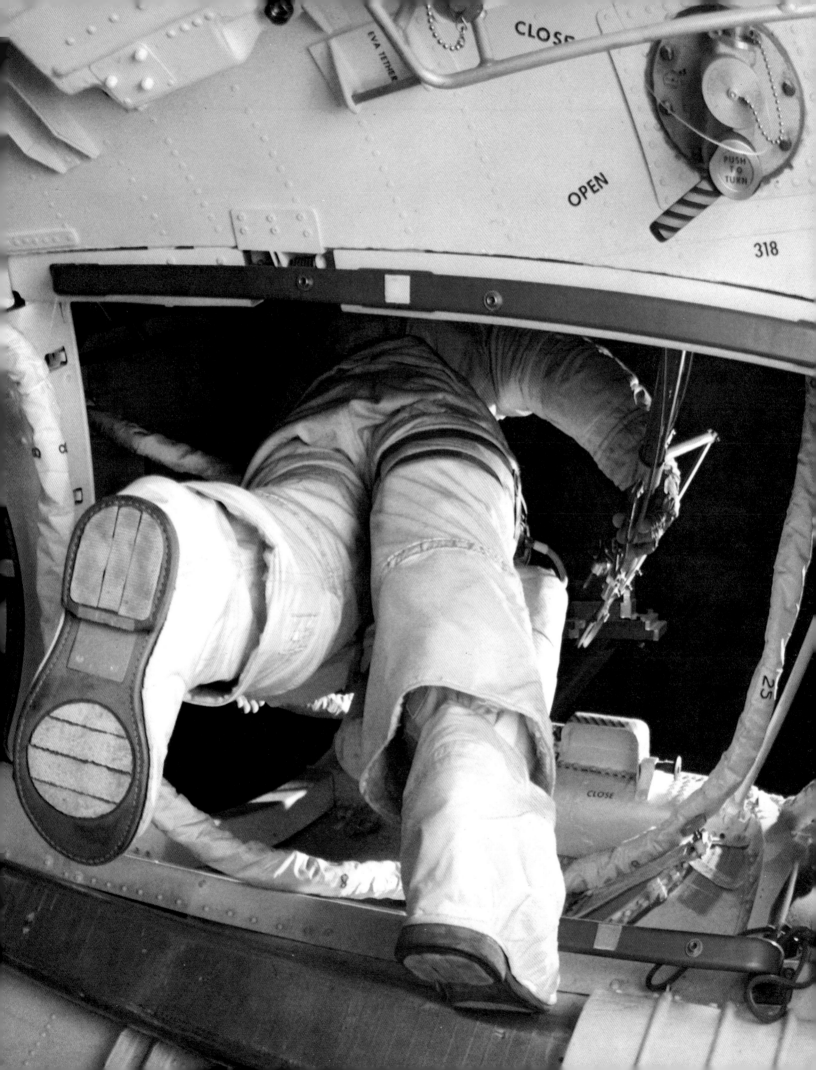

Preceding pages: In this sequence which takes the viewer through the Multiple Docking Adapter, which a Skylab astronaut described as "a very good example of how not to design and arrange a compartment," we continue into the Airlock Module, then seemingly follow an astronaut out of the Airlock Module and into space.

began to restore the muscle tissue, calcium, red corpuscles, and so on, it had lost. What was known so far was only that the more time an astronaut spent in space, the poorer the condition he seemed to be in upon his return. NASA flight surgeons were also aware that in 1970 two Soviet cosmonauts had been so weakened after spending eighteen days in orbit that they had to be carried from their spacecraft on stretchers upon landing. Even more ominous was the mystery surrounding the three other Soviet cosmonauts who had spent twenty-five days in space in 1971—longer than any other men. All three of the cosmonauts had died upon returning to Earth, as a result of a vent valve having popped open. Despite this, Skylab's first crew was scheduled to exceed by three days the dead cosmonauts' record duration flight.

The Skylab crews variously described their space station as "the cluster" or "the can"— what it was, actually, was a cluster of cans. The biggest "can," Skylab's Orbital Workshop (OWS), is on display in the Space Hall. It is a back-up vehicle for the one that was orbited. The OWS, with its huge single solar wing protruding from it like a giant sail, can be reached from the balcony overlooking the Space Hall. The visitor enters the lower level of the two-deck workshop, which contains the crew quarters, food preparation and dining area, washroom, and waste processing and disposal facilities. The upper portion contains a large work-activity area, water-storage tanks, food freezers, the film vault, and experimental equipment. The upper and lower decks were divided by an open-grid partition. The astronauts tended to prefer the lower deck since it contained the most domestic-seeming rooms. The wardroom, situated here, was the astronauts' favorite place, because it contained Skylab's only large window.

...When the astronauts were [at the big wardroom window] the earth appeared dynamic and alive. It was the view from [there] that convinced all nine Skylab astronauts that the

earth had to be observed directly, as any living object should be, with all the flexibility and intelligence that a man could provide....Part of the earth was always framed now in the round window, as though the astronauts were looking through the aperture of a microscope at a living tissue—all greens, blues, yellows, and browns. "I gained a whole new feeling for the world," Gibson [Edward G. Gibson, Third Skylab crew science pilot] told a visitor after he came back. "It's God's creation put before us, and whether you are looking at a bit of it through a microscope, or most of it from space, you still have to see it to appreciate it." Like the sun, the earth was an ever-changing kaleidoscope. [William R.] Pogue [Third Skylab crew pilot] said when he was back in Houston, "Every pass was different. It was never the same orbit to orbit. The clouds were always different, the light was different. The earth was dynamic; snow would fall, rain would fall—you could never depend on freezing any image in your mind."

The most direct view of all was from *outside* the space station, where an astronaut felt there was nothing between him and what he was looking at—as though he had slipped down the barrel of the microscope and was walking about the slide, magnifying glass in hand. "Boy, if this isn't the great outdoors!" Gibson said the first time he went out. "Inside, you're just looking out through a window. Here, you're right in it." And [Jack R.] Lousma [Second Skylab crew pilot] had said after his return, "...When you're inside looking out the window...it's like being inside a train; you can't get your head around that flat pane of glass. But if you stand outdoors, on the workshop, it's like being on the front end of a locomotive as it's going down the track! But there's no noise, no vibration; everything's silent and motionless; there are no vibrations going through your feet, no wires moving, nothing flapping." Skylab was moving down the track so fast that Lousma had actually *seen* the earth roll slowly beneath him; it was so big, though, that he could barely make out its curvature unless he was looking at the horizon.

...All the astronauts who went up [the scaffolding of the telescope tower to what the astronauts called the sun end] agreed that the sun end was the most exhilarating place aboard Skylab. "To be on the end of the telescope mount, hanging by your feet as you plunge into darkness, when you can't see your hands in front of your face—you see nothing but flashing thunderstorms and stars—that's one of the minutes I'd like to recapture and remember forever," Lousma had said afterward. It was a

During re-entry Skylab 4's exterior was subjected to temperatures of 2800°C. (5000°F). To protect it, the Command Module was covered with a 3,000-pound ablative heat shield composed of a phenolic epoxy resin in a Fiberglas honeycomb structure. The heat was carried away from the spacecraft as the heat shield charred and vaporized in friction with the earth's atmosphere.

little unnerving, too. When Pogue went up, he had the uneasy feeling that comes with being in the crow's nest of a ship. The telescope tower didn't sway like a ship's mast; it was just that an astronaut up there was far enough away from any large structure that he no longer felt part of the space station.

—*A House in Space*, by Henry S.F. Cooper, Jr.

At the forward end of the Skylab Orbital Workshop was a shorter, narrower "can" approximately the size of an Apollo spacecraft; this was the Airlock Module (AM). Because of the size of the Skylab "cluster of cans," the Airlock Module is displayed in the Space Hall horizontally next to the Orbital Workshop. In its orbit configuration, the AM rests atop the OWS, and further above the AM came the Multiple Docking Adapter, at the end of which the Apollo spacecraft ferrying up the crews would dock.

The Airlock Module (the back-up module for the one used) can be viewed by the visitor from all sides. The AM made it possible for Skylab astronauts to go outside the OWS without dispersing the Skylab's interior

atmosphere into space. The astronaut would put on his space suit, enter the AM, and close the hatch connecting the module to the OWS. He would then vent the Airlock Module's atmosphere and, when pressure in the airlock reached zero, he could open the hatch and float out into space, as the mannequin in this exhibit appears to be doing. The Airlock Module contained the control panels for the atmosphere and temperature for the entire Skylab; it also distributed electrical power throughout the Skylab cluster and supported communications and data handling. The importance of the AM was proven with the first Skylab crew, who had to carry out vital emergency repairs on the exterior of the Skylab after one of the huge solar wings and insulation had been lost during the launch. The Skylab astronauts regularly emerged from their spacecraft to replace or adjust equipment, change film, or carry out other extra vehicular activities.

The Multiple Docking Adapter (MDA) provided docking facilities for the Apollo Command and Service Modules (CSM) carrying the three-astronaut crews. In addition to the docking hatch at the end, a side docking hatch was provided in case of emergency so that two CSMs could dock simultaneously. The design of the Multiple Docking Adapter infuriated the third crew's Pogue; in fact, of the nine astronauts, only Gibson actually liked to be in the MDA. Because the MDA was a long tunnel with consoles, instruments, and boxes radiating from its cylindrical walls, there was no clear vertical and the astronauts had a hard time orienting themselves inside it. Pogue exploded, "Well, all I gotta say is, if you want a very good example of how not to design and arrange a compartment, the docking adapter is the best example. Boy, it's so lousy, I don't even want to talk about it until I get back down to the ground, because every time I think about how stupid the layout is in there, I get all upset!" Gibson's attraction for the MDA was that it was where the solar console was. After receiving his doctorate in physics from Cal Tech and writing a book about the sun, Gibson had become an astronaut because he knew that that was the only way he would see the sun from above the Earth's atmosphere. Sun watching was one of the astronauts' favorite pastimes. And the Apollo Telescope Mount's eight astronomical instruments, which were designed to observe the sun over a wide spectrum from visible light to X-rays, fed their images to the control and display console in the Multiple Docking Adapter.

All three Skylab missions were highly successful. The astronauts' tasks—to observe the Earth, using a variety of techniques designed to further knowledge of natural resources and the Earth's environment; to observe the sun for increased understanding of solar processes and influences on Earth's environment; to conduct experiments in processing materials under the unique conditions of weightlessness and the vacuum of space—were carried out with such gratifying results that the data and photographs obtained will be under analysis for years.

Most important, however, was the successful experiment conducted by and on the astronauts themselves, for they proved that man:

> . . . is a more adaptable creature and space a more suitable home for him than anyone had previously expected.
> The chief worry, though, was one trend that had not stabilized in space at all: the slow, steady loss of calcium from the astronauts' bones, which had gotten progressively worse the longer they had been weightless. This was the only area in which the two later crews were worse off than the first, and it was the trend that took the longest to right itself after their return.
> After the astronauts' bone calcium had returned to normal, there was no way a flight surgeon could tell by any clinical test that any of them had ever been in space. Yet as much as six or eight weeks after their return, the astronauts' wives reported, they stumbled at night in the dark, evidently requiring a visual clue to the room's vertical even though their sense of balance had completely returned to normal. And for a long time afterward some of the astronauts kept trying to float things around them as they had done in the space

station. One morning when he was shaving, Lousma tried to leave his can of shaving cream hovering in midair. It crashed to the floor.
> —*A House in Space,*
> by Henry S. F. Cooper, Jr.

The third and last Skylab crew departed from it on February 8, 1974, after occupying it for 84 days. Astronauts Carr, Gibson, and Pogue; Bean, Garriott, and Lousma; and Conrad, Kerwin, and Weitz had lived inside the space station for a total of 171 days, orbited the Earth 2,476 times, and traveled some 70,500,000 miles. As their Apollo Command Module, Skylab 4, undocked and pulled away from Skylab abandoning it forever, Gibson radioed, "It's been a good home."

Five years after the last Skylab mission the 77.5-ton space station's orbit began to deteriorate faster than expected due to unexpectedly high sunspot activity; and on July 11, 1979, those few parts of the Skylab that did not burn up in the atmosphere or plunge into the Indian Ocean came crashing down in Western Australia near Perth. Sheep rancher John Seiler and his wife Elizabeth were jolted awake after midnight at the isolated sheep ranch 480 miles east of Perth by a great noise and rushed outside. Seiler reported, "It was an incredible sight— hundreds of shining lights dropping all around the homestead. They were white, but as they began dropping the pieces turned dull red. All the time there was a tremendous sonic boom." As pieces of the huge satellite whizzed overhead, Seiler said his horses and cattle were terrified. "It was like a windmilling sound, quite frightening. The dogs barked and went wild when the sonic booms followed. Then there were thumps— they must have been the biggest pieces crashing down. Finally, the house shook three times. Afterward there was a burning smell."

In 1962, when John Glenn, the first American to orbit earth, passed over Perth, the city had turned on all its lights to greet him. Ironically seventeen years later NASA's plunging Skylab unintentionally returned the compliment.

Apollo–Soyuz Test Project

On July 17, 1975, a few minutes after noon in Washington, D.C., and seven PM in Moscow, a 32-foot long silver Apollo Command and Service Module with an especially constructed ten-foot long Docking Module at its nose nudged gently closer to the smaller, pale-green Soviet Soyuz-19 spacecraft drifting in orbit 140 miles above the west coast of Portugal over the Atlantic. The Soyuz had been launched two days earlier from Tyuratam about 2,000 miles southeast of the Soviet capital at 3:20 PM Moscow time with cosmonauts Aleksey A. Leonov and Valeriy N. Kubasov inside. About seven-and-a-half hours later, at 3:50 PM Washington time (EDT), a Saturn 1B carrying the Apollo Command and Service Module plus Docking Module and with astronauts Thomas P. Stafford, Donald K. ("Deke") Slayton, and Vance D. Brand aboard had thundered aloft from Cape Kennedy, in Florida.

"Less than five meters distance," Apollo commander Stafford announced now in Russian. Although he was speaking to the Soviet cosmonauts inside their spacecraft, observers around the world could listen in and watch on their television screens as the Apollo made its slow and delicate approach. Against the black background of space, were it not for the Russian spacecraft's extended solar panels, * the Soyuz appeared like a flying eggcup. "...Three meters," Stafford said in

---

*The top of the Soyuz "eggcup" was the Orbital Module; 8.7 feet long and 9 feet at its widest, the Orbital Module was used by the crew for work and rest. The 7.2-foot long inverted cup-shaped Descent Module, which came next, contained the main controls and couches used by the crew during launch, descent, and landing. The final section, the 7.5-foot long Instrument Module, held the subsystems for power, communications, propulsion, and other functions. The 28-foot long solar panels extended from this module and were used to convert sunshine to electricity to recharge the Soyuz spacecraft's batteries. The Apollo's electrical systems were powered by fuel cells which generated electricity by chemical means.

Russian, "...one meter...." The two spacecrafts' reciprocal docking mechanisms touched. "Contact!"

"Capture!" a cosmonaut said in English.

The docking latches on the Apollo and Soyuz automatically began to hook and close; the flower petal-like guide plates in each spacecraft intertwined, clasped like fingers.

"We also have capture," confirmed Stafford, his Russian colored by an Oklahoma twang.

Cosmonaut Leonov added, "Soyuz and Apollo are shaking hands now." The two spacecraft were locked together as one while Western Europe slid beneath them.

"Close active hooks," Stafford ordered, "Docking is completed." Then, in English for the benefit of the Apollo ground controllers at the Johnson Space Center, Stafford repeated, "Docking is completed, Houston."

From within the Soyuz, Houston could hear a cosmonaut's accented English, "Well done, Tom. It was a good show. We're looking forward to shaking hands with you aboard Soyuz."

The successful linkup of the two space rivals' workhorse spacecraft, the Apollo and the Soyuz, high above Earth, was the direct result of an accord reached more than three years earlier when, on May 24, 1972, then-President Richard M. Nixon and Aleksey Kosygin, Chairman of the USSR Council of Ministers, signed an agreement in Moscow "concerning cooperation in the exploration and use of outer space for peaceful purposes." This agreement establishing the Apollo-Soyuz Test Project that was designed to develop and fly a standardized docking system "to enhance the safety of manned flight in space and to provide the opportunity for conducting joint missions in space," was the result of meetings and discussions already carried out by representatives of the two nations for several years. There had then followed three years of intense training, and the setting up of an elaborate communications network to make it possible for Houston and Kaliningrad controllers to be in constant touch with their spacecraft and each other. Engineers in this country and the Soviet Union designed and built the necessary docking hardware which would enable the two incompatible spacecraft with different atmospheric pressures to become one. The astronauts and the cosmonauts, engineers and technicians and interpreters from both sides spent hundreds of hours in joint training and in attempts to learn each other's language. Two-fifths-size scale models of the docking systems developed by both nations were constructed on wheeled tables and pushed together to see if they joined. They did. And the compatible docking systems now made possible a variety of projects involving manned spacecraft from the Soviet Union and the United States such as internationally manned space stations, in addition to showing that an international rescue operation could be carried out should one nation have a stranded spacecraft in orbit and no rescue vessel from its own country ready to be launched to bring down an imperiled crew.

About three hours after the orbiting Soyuz and Apollo had docked, persons gathered at Apollo Control in Houston and Soyuz Control at Kaliningrad watched their television monitors. On their screens the pipelike interior of the Docking Module ended in the still-closed hatch connecting the two spacecraft. Two American astronauts, the shoulders of their brown-gold space "fatigues" occasionally crowding into the screen, were continuing down their checklist:

"Soyuz, our step 23 is completed," called one of the astronauts into the intercom. He was informing the two-man crew in the adjoining Soyuz of his progress. "We are now working on step 24." He spoke in Russian.

"We're through with that, too," said the second astronaut. "Right here 25. Let me get the light on....Camera. Yep, we're right on schedule. Okay there."

The dialogue by the Americans came through loud and clear at Houston. In numerous training sessions the American and Russian ground personnel had become thoroughly acquainted with the steps involved in opening the passageway from one spacecraft into another.

"Okay to unlock?"

"The camera is running," interjected the unseen third U.S. crew member who was in the Apollo Command Module.

"Right on schedule," repeated the first astronaut, glancing at his wristwatch.

"Hatch opening," shouted the second astronaut.

Thus at 2:17 PM Houston Time (3:17 PM Washington Time), 10:17 PM Moscow Time, hatch number 3 swung open removing the last barrier between a U.S. and U.S.S.R. spacecraft. The U.S. TV camera that had been aiming at the hatch was now looking straight through the cylindrical passageway into the Soviet Soyuz. There the TV picture first showed some tangled, spaghetti-like communications cables.

"Looks like they've got a few snakes in there too," said the first American who had just disengaged himself from strands of unruly cable floating weightlessly in the Docking Module.

Then the TV screen showed movement at the far end of the passageway and the face and body of the Soyuz crew commander appeared. He was dressed in a flight garment similar to the garments worn by the Americans. He stretched his arm forward through the passageway where his hand was clasped by the American crew commander.

"Glad to see you," said the Russian in English with only a trace of an accent.

Thus two veteran space explorers—U.S. Air Force Brigadier General Thomas P. Stafford, an astronaut since 1962* and Soviet Air Force Colonel Aleksey A. Leonov, a cosmonaut since 1960**—met in Earth orbit.

As Leonov and Stafford held on to each other momentarily, their arms and hands formed a symbolic bridge between their nations. At last, the two nations in the endeavor—the only ones

---

*Prior to Apollo-Soyuz, Stafford had made three flights in space; his first had been in Gemini 6, December 15–16, 1965; then Gemini 9, June 3–6, 1966; his third flight, aboard Apollo 10, was the dress rehearsal for a lunar landing with the lunar module dropping down to nine miles from the moon.

**During Voshkod 2's 17-orbit flight on March 18, 1965, Leonov had made the world's first "space walk."

24 feet

Exhaust cone of main propulsion system.

Apollo Service Module which

├── 43 feet ──┤

ed the main propulsion system, supplies, and equipment.

*Apollo Command Module in which
the astronauts lived. It was the only
section to return from space; it
contained the spacecraft's controls.*

— 66 feet —

The Docking Module carried into space by the Apollo crew through which the American and Soviet crews could pass to each others' spacecraft.

Docking mechanism in its hard-dock position.

Soyuz Orbital Module, used by the Soviet crew for work and rest during the mission.

Descent Module which was equipped
with main controls and couches used
during launch, descent, and landing.

Instrument Module which contained subsystems for power
communications, propulsion, and other functions. The solar
panels extending from its sides supplied electricity to
recharge the Soyuz' batteries.

so far to have flown men in space*—were working together rather than separately as they had through most of the period since the space age opened nearly 18 years earlier.

—*Apollo Soyuz*, by Walter Froehlich

For the next two days the crews of the Apollo and Soyuz shared meals, exchanged gifts and mementoes, conducted scientific experiments, but most of all provided the world with a vivid demonstration of detente on the way to achieving a series of "firsts": in addition to conducting the first space flight and docking of spacecraft and crews of different nations, Apollo-Soyuz detected the first pulsar outside our own galaxy, and the first stars emitting extreme-ultraviolet radiation (one of which is the hottest "white dwarf" known); the first separation of live biologic materials in space by electro-phoresis was achieved; and for the first time communications between a manned orbiting spacecraft and ground controllers was carried out via an orbiting unmanned communications satellite.

Although among the millions of viewers in many different parts of the world who watched the live telecasts there were doubtless many who shrugged the Apollo-Soyuz project off as "nothing but a glittering soap bubble"—as did the West Berlin newspaper *Spandauer Volksblatt*, or regretted, like the Copenhagen *Jyllands-Posten*, the joint project's 450-million-dollar cost which prompted "reflection on how much the world's two biggest superpowers could achieve if they agreed to mobilize their strength and technology in joint service of more close-to-earth causes,"—no one would disagree with the London *Sun*'s perception that "It was the world's most expensive handshake, but it will not have cost a dollar or ruble too much if it is a handclasp for peace."

At the very least, the Apollo-Soyuz Test Project was a dramatic demonstration on the part of both the United States and the Soviet Union of a willingness to relax tension. Perhaps when spacecraft in the future establish the first extra-terrestrial colony, when international laboratories are orbited, when colonization of space occurs, Apollo-Soyuz will be remembered as a footnote: the first truly international manned space venture. As NASA's director for Apollo-Soyuz, Chester M.Lee said at the time,"Space is going to be explored. It's man's inherent nature to do that, and we might as well do it together."

The Apollo-Soyuz flight was the last Apollo launch and the last American manned space flight using a disposable spacecraft and launch vehicle.

---

*Even as Soyuz and Apollo met, two Soviet cosmonauts were aboard a Soviet Salyut space station. Salyut 6, a space station launched in September, 1977, has now been visited by cosmonauts from Czechoslovakia (Vladimir Remek, March, 1978), Poland (Miroslaw Hermaszewki, July, 1978), and East Germany (Sigmund Jahn, August, 1978).

The Space Shuttle

135

Ever since 1957 when the Space Age began, space transportation has depended upon launch vehicles that are used just once and discarded. Arthur C. Clarke compared the economic sense made by this policy to the owners of the Cunard Line building the Queen Elizabeth, sending it across the Atlantic with three passengers, and then, after they disembarked, willingly sinking the ship. The concept of a fully recoverable space transportation vehicle of one or two stages has obviously therefore been under study for years.

During the mid- and late-1960s the "lifting body" or wingless aircraft concept was one of several approaches taken toward solving the problems of aerodynamic heating and vehicle control during reentry from Earth orbit—problems of critical importance in the success of the Space Shuttle of the 1980s, which will have to operate through a wide range of speeds. The blunt-nosed, wingless M2-F3 Lifting Body suspended in the Space Hall and shown in this chapter derived its lift from its fuselage. Although removing the wings reduced the weight of a craft, it added significant problems of control and stability. The May 10, 1967, crash of an M2-F2 test vehicle forerunner of the M2-F3 was partly due to control instability later cured by the addition on the M2-F3 of a central fin. (This crash can be seen weekly behind the introduction and credits of the popular television series, *The Six Million Dollar Man*; unlike the bionic TV character, however, the actual test pilot suffered the loss of one eye.) The M2 test program proved that a wingless craft could operate through

subsonic, transonic, and supersonic speeds, and that a shuttle vehicle could make unpowered approaches and landings, paving the way for the Space Shuttle design.

One of the most provoking exhibits, however, is the Lunar Base Concept model *Counterpoint* constructed by J.R. Dossey and G.L. Trotti for an undergraduate thesis in architecture at the University of Houston in Texas. *Counterpoint* is designed to be a fully independent lunar colony with about 200 inhabitants and would be located in the St. George Crater, near Apollo 15's landing site. But the visitor should keep in mind that the space stations, lunar bases, and Mars missions shown in this part of the gallery are all concepts considered technologically possible now and could become national or international programs before the century ends. And by that time, of course, it will be *2001*. Really.

The M2-F3 "Lifting Body" was designed to
test flight behavior of wingless craft over a
wide range of speeds. The M2-F3 achieved
its aerodynamic lift from the shape of its body.

At a little before 7 A.M. on April 12, 1981 at Cape Canaveral, Florida, space shuttle commander John W. Young and pilot Robert L. Crippen were waiting inside the cockpit of the *Columbia,* the first U. S. manned spacecraft ever to be launched without having undergone prior unmanned test flights in space. Already two years behind schedule and 3.6 billion dollars over budget, the *Columbia* was to carry the first U. S. astronauts into space since the Apollo-Soyuz link-up six years before.

The *Columbia,* the world's first reusable manned-space vehicle, is the most complex flying machine ever built. Its three main space shuttle engines would have to provide 375,000 pounds of lift, deal with unprecedented pressures and operate at greater temperature extremes than any mechanical system in common use today. In early tests of the space shuttle engines, seals had burst, propellant lines ruptured, valves had blown, faulty welds gave way, turbine blades cracked, ball bearings splintered, engines had exploded. The three main space shuttle engines develop just over 37-million horsepower and release an energy equivalent to that of 23 Hoover Dams. During launch and ascent these engines consume a half-million gallons of liquid-hydrogen fuel in about eight and a half minutes. It was not until 1980 that the space shuttle main engines, under development since 1972 (when an unenthusiastic President had asked a skeptical Congress to authorize inadequate funds for the space shuttle program), were pronounced ready for flight. By then it had already been discovered that thousands of the 30,761 tiles—each eccentrically shaped and unique, ranging in size from six-by-six inches to the palm of one's hand—would not withstand the rigors of a 17,100 mph reentry from space and would have to be reattached. In fact, some 7,500 tiles had been lost or damaged during the comparatively smooth flight of the *Columbia* when it was piggybacked from the West Coast to Cape Canaveral on top of a special Boeing 747. The loss of any single tile during reentry could lead to a general irreversible burnout and the deaths of the crew. It took two years for the problems with the tiles to be resolved.

Despite these difficulties, however, there was reason on launch day to be optimistic. The *Columbia* is the most versatile and ambitious spacecraft ever developed and it stood against its launch gantry on Pad 39A glistening with promise. Before the space shuttle, everything was carried into space by expendable, one-time-only launch vehicles. The *Columbia,* which takes off like a rocket, operates in orbit like a spacecraft, and lands like a glider, was designed to make space flight routine. Shuttle flights are expected to happen so frequently as to be regularly scheduled. NASA hopes that the *Columbia,* and the three other versions now in production, will give the U. S. a commuter-service capability into space during the 1980s. NASA officials envision the shuttle as a back-and-forth pick-up truck whose 65,000-pound cargo hold can put a space lab into position, manned and ready, or orbit a 22,500-pound space telescope as well as carry up satellites and other payloads for science, the military and industry. The shuttle is expected to be the first practical step toward the industrialization of space. Because the shuttle is reusable, the investment required to build it can be spread over an extended lifetime, a period during which NASA intends to put some 200 Americans in orbit—somewhat optimistically—by the end of 1987. But, as April 12, 1981 dawned with astronauts Young and Crippen sitting strapped in *Columbia's* cockpit watching the pelicans fly up and down the beach while the countdown for launch continued, all the hopes and expectations for America's shuttle program were compressed into the here and now: would the launch be scrubbed? Would the mission, once launched, have to abort? Would there be problems in orbit? Would the tiles withstand reentry?

In order for the mission to succeed, all three main elements of the space shuttle

The huge transporters which carry the Space Shuttle from the Vehicle Assembly Building to the launch pad are large enough for a major-league infield and each individual link of tread weighs one ton.

with its thousands of parts had to function together and in their proper sequence. There was the *Columbia* Orbiter, a delta-winged aircraft-spacecraft about the length of a twin jet commercial airliner, but far bulkier and built to be reused for at least 100 flights; the dirigible-like expendable External Tank; and, attached to the sides of the External Tank, two reusable Solid Rocket Boosters, each longer and fatter than a railway tank car. By T-minus-five minutes the astronauts were too busy with last-minute launch preparations to enjoy the Cape Canaveral dawn. Here, in the astronauts' own words, is how the first shuttle flight went. Pilot Robert L. Crippen speaks first; the story is then picked up by shuttle commander John W. Young.

Crippen: *It wasn't until we hit T-minus-27 seconds and nothing had gone wrong that I made up my mind we were really going to do it. That's when my heart rate went up to 130. I'm surprised it wasn't higher. John, I guess, was calmer. He had been into space four times and walked on the moon.* Maybe that's why his heart rate was only about 85.*

Young: I was excited too. I just couldn't get my heart to beat any faster. I was pretty impressed anyway, when at T minus five seconds I heard the three main engines start up with bangs. Then the two solid rocket boosters, which were strapped onto our big white external tank, exploded to life. Within three-tenths of a second we were off the ground. I saw pictures later of the conflagration all those engines and boosters made. I'm sure glad we didn't have rearview mirrors.

Looking out the side windows, I watched the vehicle go by the tower. There was a little vibration at first, and much less noise than I expected. Basically it was smooth, like riding a fast elevator . . . .

We launched with *Columbia's* tail

facing south. Immediately after clearing the tower, we did this roll, pitch and yaw maneuver to get ourselves headed east-northeast toward Gibraltar.

We were getting more thrust from those solid rockets than we expected. When we jettisoned the solids, for instance, we were supposed to be at 164,000 feet, but were already at 174,000.

Those solids were putting out a tail of flame that was more than 600 feet long and 200 feet wide. Photographs from the chase planes show the flames were so hot that the back of the external tank was glowing bright white. We were about to lose the solids, however. We could feel a slight deceleration; their fuel was just about spent. Then two minutes and 11 seconds after lift-off when we were 29 nautical miles high, there was bright yellow-orange flame all across our windows. Six-tenths of a second later it was gone, and so were the solid rockets. Eight booster separator motors had flared up and fired the solids off into the Atlantic. That was some flash. We weren't expecting it to be so breath-taking, but for six-tenths of a second you don't have time to get nervous.

Crippen: *About two minutes later we were feeling good. All our testing data had indicated that if the engines were going to fail, they'd have done it already. Then we got the call from Mission Control in Houston we'd been waiting for: "Press to MECO." MECO, or main engine cutoff, occurs just before we reach orbital velocity. If we were cleared to go that far, we knew we weren't going to have to turn around and come back.*

At this point, right on schedule, Columbia suddenly pitched over to level off our trajectory. As it did, I saw earth from space for the first time. "What a view! What a view!" was all I could get out. Seeing that curvature of the earth against the black of space, the multihued ocean, and the vivid blue shimmer at the top of the atmosphere grabbed my breath. "It hasn't changed any," said John.

Young: Neither of us could sightsee, however. In less than four minutes we had to jettison the external tank. Pieces of

---

*Young had been aboard *Gemini 3, Gemini 10, Apollo 10* and, as part of *Apollo 16*, had been the ninth man to walk on the moon.

white insulation from the tank drifted by our windows. They looked spectacular, like chunks of ice.

We were flying upside down underneath the tank, to make getting away from it easier. The main engines cut off, and the computers activated a 16-second separation sequence. Our umbilical lines were pulled out of the tank back into the orbiter. Then explosives blew the bolts fastening us to the tank, and Columbia was flying free. We couldn't see the tank, but knew it was up above us and would soon begin to drift down on a trajectory that would take whatever pieces survived the heat of entering the atmosphere into the Indian Ocean.

Up in the cockpit the only way we knew we had separated from the tank was that three red lights on the panel in front of Bob Crippen went out. There was no motion, no sense of the explosives firing. I took the stick and began manually flying off to the side to guarantee that we wouldn't run into the tank as it fell.

Crippen: *Actually, it felt like we were walking away from the external tank. The orbiter has 44 reaction control engines. These thrusters, which you can fire one at a time or in tandem, let us control the direction and attitude of Columbia most of the time we were in space. They were very physical and really shook the vehicle. They sounded like muffled howitzers right outside our door. Later, when we fired them at night, we could see 30-foot-long tongues of fire leaping out from them. It was a little uncomfortable initially, and we never entirely got used to it. When one of the bigger ones fired, it was like something had hit the vehicle.*

To get away from the tank, John flew the vehicle off to one side, and the computers fired one reaction jet on the nose and one aft. The one on the nose cut off intermittently to hold attitude. That kept Columbia positioned properly, but it also made us feel as if we were sidestepping across the sky. We didn't anticipate that.

Now rid of the tank, we were busy getting ready for our next maneuver. John took the rotational hand controller and pulled up Columbia's nose. He

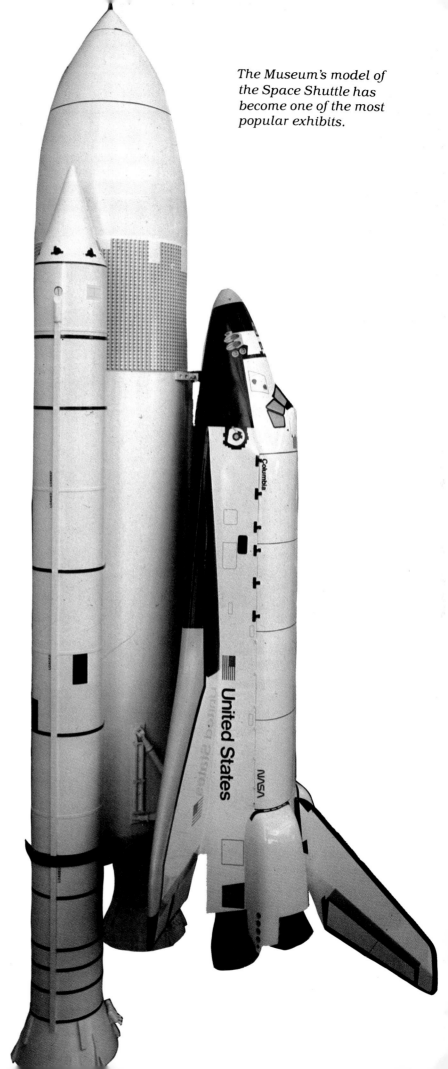

The Museum's model of the Space Shuttle has become one of the most popular exhibits.

pushed a button. The two large orbital maneuvering system (OMS) engines, which sit above the main engines at the rear of the spacecraft, fired. They gave us a smooth and silent push into orbit . . . about 20 minutes later we fired the OMS engines again to make our orbit circular, about 130 nautical miles above the earth.

Once we hit orbit, we unbuckled our seatbelts and went to work. We loaded the computers with the on-orbit programs they needed to control and monitor just about every aspect of our flight and environment. As I got up to go into the aft flight deck behind the cockpit, I really noticed my weightlessness.

Right after the main engines had cut off, we had seen a little debris—washers and screws—floating through the cockpit. But not until I unstrapped my seatbelt did I realize how spectacular weightlessness is. I felt like a bird learning to fly from its nest.

I floated to the aft deck to open the large doors that cover the payload bay. The payload doors must stay open most of the time in orbit. They have reflectors that radiate into space the heat that builds up from all the electronic equipment.

John was back there, too, feet up in the air, and getting ready to take pictures with three remotely controlled T.V. cameras located in the cargo bay.

As soon as we got the door open, I noticed some dark patches on the pod that houses the starboard OMS engine. "Hey, John," I said, "we've got some tiles missing."

We didn't know it but those missing tiles caused quite a commotion back on earth. We weren't worried. The pods weren't supposed to get that hot during reentry, and NASA was being conservative by tiling that area.

Also we could see that the red compound called RTV, which helps bond the tiles, was still there. That itself will insulate against heat up to 900 degrees. The wings and tail were OK, and they were the most critical parts of the orbiter that we could see from the windows that look out on the cargo bay.

We did not know what had happened during ascent to the really important tiles on the underbelly. But it looked to us as if the tiles we had lost had not been hit by anything. There is a complex curvature on the OMS pod, and it appeared that mechanical flexing during ascent had popped those tiles off. It seemed unlikely that that would have happened on the gentler curves on the bottom of the spacecraft.

Young: We spent most of that first day making sure Columbia was working properly. We went around checking our systems and doing routine first-flight things like surveying noise levels in the cockpit or checking the hand controller. One of us always stayed on the flight deck, since that is where the alarms and controls are. Because of zero G it was more fun to zoom down below into the mid-deck to do a checkout. Bob Crippen thought so too. He was learning how to swim in space pretty quickly.

Crippen: After I assured myself I wasn't going to get spacesick, I spent a lot of time enjoying zero G. You don't have to do fancy aerobatics. Just moving around is enough. At first I did things that surprised me, like shoving off from one side of the mid-deck a bit too hard and finding myself sprawled on the opposite wall. But I mastered it pretty quickly. Soon I felt graceful and could fully control my body and motion.

Young: We had a complex flight plan, detailing what we were to do almost minute by minute. After we finished the first day's chores, Crip fixed us dinner. Mission Control told us it was bedtime and signed off for the next eight hours. Neither one of us slept well that first night. For one thing it was light out much of the time and far too beautiful looking down at earth.

Sixteen years ago on Gemini 3 we didn't have any windows to speak of. There was one porthole in front of me and one in front of Gus Grissom. The only way we could take pictures was to point a camera straight at something or open the hatch. (We didn't do that much.) On Apollo we were on our way to the moon. We didn't have much chance to look back and take pictures. We were moving too fast anyway.

Crippen: *The shuttle has those wraparound windows up front. But the best views are from the flight deck windows, looking out through the payload bay when you are flying upside down with the doors open, which we were doing most of the time. You see the whole earth going by beneath you.*

I remember one time glancing out and there were the Himalayas, rugged, snow covered, and stark. They are usually obscured by clouds, but this day was clear and the atmosphere so thin around them that we could see incredible detail and vivid color contrast. The human eye gives you a 3-D effect no camera can. Sights like the Himalayas and thunderstorms, which we later saw billowing high above the Amazon, are especially dramatic.

Young: I wasn't ready to go to bed that first night at quitting time even though we had been up for 18 hours. I slept only three or four hours. Crip did a bit better. When we did turn in, we just fastened our lap belts and folded our arms. We could have gone down to the mid-deck and just floated around, but I like some support. Anyway you do it, sleeping in zero G is delightful. It's like being on a water bed in three dimensions.

Crippen: *We were busy most of our second day, April 13, doing burns with the reaction control jets, going into different attitudes and performing maneuvers. We needed to understand how well the computer autopilot can control the vehicle. Could we make fine maneuvers? Houston wanted to see how well the crew could coordinate with the ground in positioning the orbiter.*

Young: I just kept feeling better and better about that vehicle. After we launched and got it into orbit, I had said to myself, "Well, that went pretty good." Then the vehicle worked so well the first day I had said, "We'd better take it back before it breaks." The second day it worked even better and so I thought, "Man, this thing is really good. We'd better stay up here some more to get more data." But Mission Control made us come back the next day.

Crippen: *We both slept soundly that second night. I was really sawing the Zs when an alarm started going off in my ears. I didn't know where I was, who I was, or what I was doing for the longest time. I could hear John saying, "Crip, what's that?" It was a minor problem, fortunately. A heater control in one of our auxiliary power units quit working. We just switched on an alternate heater and went back to sleep.*

It was about 2:30 A.M. Houston time when flight control greeted us with a bugle call and some rousing music. John fixed breakfast that morning although usually I took care of the chow. Then we checked out the flight control system one last time and stowed everything away for reentry. We strapped on biomedical sensors to keep the doctors happy, and got back into our pressure suits. We programmed the computers for reentry and closed the payload bay doors.

The first step toward getting home was to de-orbit. We had tested all our engines and were very confident they were working. We were really looking forward to flying reentry. Bringing a winged vehicle down from almost 25 times the speed of sound would be a thrill for any pilot.

We were orbiting tail first and upside down. We fired the OMS engines enough to feel a nice little push that slowed us down by a little less than 300 feet per second. That is not dramatic, but it did change our orbit back to an ellipse whose low point would be close to the surface of the earth.

When we finished the OMS burn, John pitched the vehicle over so it was in the forty degree nose-up angle that would let our insulated underbelly meet the reentry heat of the atmosphere.

Young: We hit the atmosphere at the equivalent of about Mach 24.5 after passing Guam. About the same time we lost radio contact with Houston. There were no tracking stations in that part of the Pacific. Also, the heat of reentry would block radio communications for the next 16 minutes.

Just before losing contact, we noticed a slight crackling on the radio. Then, out of the sides of our eyes, we saw little blips of orange. We knew we had met the atmosphere. Those blips were the reaction control jets firing. In space we never noticed those rear jets because there were no molecules to reflect their light forward. Those blips told us that *Columbia* was coming through air—and hence, plenty of molecules to reflect the thrusters' fire.

That air was also creating friction and heating *Columbia*'s exterior. About five minutes after we lost contact with Houston, at the beginning of reentry heating, when we were still flying at Mach 24.5, we noticed the reddish-pink glow. Bob and I put our visors down. That sealed our pressure suits so that they would automatically inflate if somehow reentry heating burned through the cabin and let the air out. Other than the pink glow, however, we had no sense of going through a hot phase.

Crippen: *Columbia was flying smoother than any airliner. Not a ripple!*

As we approached the coast of northern California we were doing Mach 7 and I could pick out Monterey Bay. We were about to enter the most uncertain part of our flight. Up to this point, Columbia's course was controlled largely by firings of its reaction control thrusters. But as the atmosphere grew denser, the thrusters became less effective. Columbia's aerodynamic controls, such as its elevons and rudder, began to take over.

We had more and more air building up on the vehicle, and we were going far faster than any winged vehicle had ever flown. Moreover, the thrusters were still firing. It was an approach with a lot of unknowns. Wind tunnels just cannot test such complex aerodynamics well. That was the main reason John took control of the flight from the automated system at a little under Mach 5. We had been doing rolls, using them a little like a skier uses turns to slow and control descent down a mountain. The flight plan called for John to fly the last two rolls manually. He would fly them more smoothly than the automatic system, helping to avoid excessive sideslipping and ensuring that we would not lose control as we came down the middle of our approach corridor.

The Space Telescope, will be able to see objects fifty times fainter than the best ground-based telescopes. It will be placed in orbit by the Space Shuttle, whose crew will be able to service and repair the telescope as the need arises.

Young: It turned out to be totally unnecessary for me to manually fly those last two roll reversals. *Columbia* had been flying like a champ. It has all those sensors: platforms for attitude control, gyroscopes, and accelerometers. Its computers take all the data, assimilate it instantly, and use it to fire thrusters, drive elevons, or do anything needed to fly the vehicle. They are much faster at this than any man. The orbiter is a joy to fly. It does what you tell it to, even in very unstable regions. All I had to do was say, "I want to roll right," or "Put my nose here," and it did it. The vehicle went where I wanted it, and it stayed there until I moved the control stick to put it somewhere else.

Crippen: *Flying down the San Joaquin Valley exhilarated me. What a way to come to California! Visibility was perfect. Given some airspeed and altitude information, we could have landed visually.*

John did his last roll reversal at Mach 2.6. The thrusters had stopped firing by then, and we shifted into an all-aerodynamic mode. We found out later that we had made a double sonic boom as we slowed below the speed of sound. We made a gliding circle over our landing site, runway 23 on Rogers Dry Lake at Edwards Air Force Base.

On final approach I was reading out the airspeeds to John so he wouldn't have to scan the instruments as closely. Columbia almost floated in. John only had to make minor adjustments in pitch. We were targeted to touch down at 185 knots, and the very moment I called out 185, I felt us touch down. I

have never been in any flying vehicle that landed more smoothly. If you can imagine the smoothest landing you've ever had in an airliner, ours was at least that good. John really greased it in.

"Welcome home, Columbia," said Houston. "Beautiful, beautiful."

"Do you want us to take it up to the hangar?" John asked.

—"Our Phenomenal First Flight," by John Young and Robert Crippen, *National Geographic*, October, 1981

On November 12, 1981, the space shuttle *Columbia* with Colonel Joe H. Engle, USAF, and Captain Richard H. Truly, USN, on board was launched from Pad 39A at Cape Canaveral, Florida for the second time. Due to the failure of one of the craft's three fuel cells on its first day of flight, *Columbia* was forced to carry out a shortened mission and it landed 36 orbits, two days, six hours and 13 minutes after lift-off. The original goal was a mission lasting 124 hours and 83 orbits. Despite the mechanical difficulties which necessitated the abbreviated mission, NASA officials pronounced the second flight of the *Columbia* a success.

By cramming in a heavy work load the astronauts managed to achieve all the mission's major objectives which included testing a robot arm for handling payloads in space and conducting the first scientific observations from the world's first reusable spacecraft.

Exploring
the
Planets

After ancient man learned to search both philosophically and actually beyond the Sun and Moon which dominated his heavens, he discovered that five particular objects in the nighttime sky moved against the seemingly fixed patterns of the stars and were, therefore, in some fundamental way, different from them. Once identified, they named these objects after gods: Mercury, Venus, Mars, Jupiter, and Saturn. Because of their comparative nearness, these planets were thought to move around the Earth like the Sun and the Moon. Ptolemy (C.A.D. 90-168), who perfected a system to describe their movements, placed the Earth at the center of the universe with the bodies in the following order moving in perfectly circular orbits about it: the Moon, Mercury, Venus, the Sun, Mars, Jupiter, and Saturn. And to account for observable irregularities in their orbits, each body also performed an epicycle—a small circular orbit within the circumference of the large orbit. Although several early Greek philosophers, Aristarchus (310-230 B.C.) in particular, had suggested that the Earth moved about the Sun, and not the other way around, this heliocentric theory was rejected until the Polish astronomer Nicolaus Copernicus (1473-1543) published as he lay dying his *De Revolutionibus Orbium Coelestium* containing his argument that the Sun was the center of the universe and all the planets revolved around it. So controversial and dangerous was this concept that it prompted the German theologian and leader of the Protestant Reformation Martin Luther (1483-1546) to protest, "The fool will turn the whole science of astronomy upside down!" Pope Paul III swiftly proclaimed Copernicus' theory to be heresy; but the courageous and inventive Italian scientist Galileo Galilei (1564-1642), his new telescope's discovery of Jupiter's four largest moons providing what he considered to be proof, published his support of the Copernican view of the universe in *Sidereus Nuncius.*

The telescope helped transform astronomy from a science dominated by theologic and philosophic reservations and reasoning to a pure science within the expanding realms of mathematicians and geographers. For two thousand years the only known bodies in the Solar System had been the Earth, its Moon, the Sun and the five nearest planets; now, in the seventeenth century, through Galileo's invention nine new bodies were added: the four moons of Jupiter that Galileo had discovered, and five moons of Saturn found by others.

During the next century a sixth planet, Uranus, was discovered along with two of its moons, and Saturn's sixth and seventh satellites.

On January 1, 1801, the planetoid Ceres was discovered where a planet "should" have been: in the vast empty space between the orbits of Jupiter and Mars. Within the next six years three more planetoids were discovered in what came to be known as the asteroid belt. The nineteenth century abounded in discovery; in 1846 Neptune was found and immediately thereafter one of its two moons. In 1848 Saturn's eighth satellite was discovered, in 1877 two tiny moons orbiting Mars, in 1892 a fifth satellite of Jupiter, in 1898 Saturn's ninth.

So far in the twentieth century eleven more satellites of Jupiter have been discovered; in 1948 a Dutch-American astronomer Gerard P. Kuiper discovered a fifth and innermost satellite of Uranus and in 1950 a second moon of Neptune. In 1930, with the help of Percival Lowell's computations of where just such an object might be found, Clyde W. Tombaugh discovered the ninth planet in our solar system and called it Pluto since, like the Underworld god after whom it was named, it was the farthest removed from the light.

The first exhibits in Exploring the Planets introduce this earthbound view of our solar system and show how Renaissance and Modern Man's expanding knowledge based on observable fact forced fantastic and superstitious explanations of natural phenomena to give way. Astronomers in the centuries since the telescope's invention have been able to detect objects so distant that their light began its journey to the telescopes' lenses before the Earth was even formed. Still, the great mysteries remain unsolved: How was the universe formed? Is it expanding from its creation? How long will it last? When did it begin? Are there millions of planets circling millions of stars? This last question suggests the greatest riddle of them all: Are we alone? No telescope can detect anything so small as a planet orbiting even the nearest star.

But now, as we enter the last quarter of the twentieth century, we enter a new era as well, an era which began, really, with Russia's 1959 Luna 1 mission past the Moon. As this era of manned and unmanned spacecraft exploration progresses our knowledge of the planets, their satellites, the Moon and the Sun has multiplied enormously with each successive flight. This new knowledge and the wonderful devices which have helped us achieve it, are the core of the Exploring the Planets gallery.

Visitors are shown the possible types of missions or trajectories used: flyby, impact, orbit, landing, and landing with return. A series of photographs taken by Ranger 9 demonstrates the flight attitude, descent, and crash of that craft on the Moon's surface in March, 1965. A model Surveyor sits surrounded by a lunar landscape photo mosaic created from the pictures sent back by the 1968 Surveyor 7. Here, too, is Surveyor 3's camera which the crew of Apollo 12 brought back with them from the surface of the Moon.

Visitors are shown how Mariner 9 (1971) mapped the surface of Mars and discovered that the erosional and volcanic landforms on that planet far outscale anything to be found on Earth: the great Martian volcano, *Olympus Mons*, for example, is over 81,000 feet high; Mt. Everest, by comparison, is but a puny 29,028 feet. That planet's enormous equatorial canyon, *Valles Marineris*, stretches nearly a third of the way around

Mars. And photographs from the Viking 1 and Viking 2 Mars landers (1976) revealed a ruddy, rocky surface and a pinkish sky.

Mariner 10's triple rendezvous with Mercury (twice in 1974, once in 1975) showed that planet to be as barren and cratered as the Moon; Russia's Venera 9 (1975) soft-landed on the planet Venus and sent back photographs of a hostile, rockstrewn landscape beneath a thick blanket of clouds. Pioneer 10 (1973) and Pioneer 11 (1974) sent back the first good photographs of Jupiter. A prototype of the Pioneer 10 spacecraft hangs in the Milestones of Flight gallery.

In late 1978 Venus was explored by two Pioneer Venus spacecraft. The first was a radar-equipped orbiter which provided the first contour map of Venus' surface; the second was a multiple probe that dropped five instrument packages down through the planet's five layers of atmosphere. The spacecraft revealed that the Venusian atmosphere, a hundred times thicker than Earth's, is continually riddled by lightning bolts and that its blanket of sulphuric acid clouds circumnavigates the surface of the planet every four days as regularly as clockwork.

But the scientific climax of our planetary space probes has had to be the two long ranging Voyager spacecraft, a prototype which dominates this gallery. The first of these marvelous spacecraft, Voyager 1, passed by Jupiter in March 1979 and was followed by Voyager 2 four months later. Not much larger than hang gliders, these seemingly fragile 1,800-pound machines stunned the world with the extraordinarily detailed photographs they sent back.

Voyager 1 which had sped past Jupiter at speeds approaching 45,000 mph radioed back from half a billion miles away the first clear photographs of Jupiter's Great Red Spot, an oval, 20,000-mile-long monumental storm that had first been observed by telescope in 1664. The storm's huge size and low temperature prevent it from losing energy and since Jupiter's topography seems to consist of atmosphere and little else (an atmosphere 10,000 times thicker than Venus') there are no solid features to affect the storm's flow which may explain the Spot's persistence. In addition Voyager 1 photographed Jupiter's four largest moons and discovered a thin ring surrounding Jupiter making it the third planet, after Saturn and Uranus, known to have this feature.

Voyager 2's rendezvous with Jupiter in July 1979 carried out an even closer reconnaissance of the four largest Jovian moons. As it first swept past Jupiter's outermost and seemingly oldest satellite, Callisto, Voyager 2's photographs revealed a quiet surface with probably more craters per square mile than any other body in the solar system. Voyager 2 then moved past Ganymede, Jupiter's largest moon (about 1½ times the size of our own) showing it to be probably composed of rock and ice; and so on to Europa, the brightest of Jupiter's moons which appears to be covered by an intricate network of icy veinlike fractures.

Voyager 1's photographs of pizza-colored Io revealed eight volcanoes erupting on its surface; Voyager 2 photographed six of those same volcanic eruptions four months later, an indication that these eruptions might be going on for years. The bright orange and yellow color of Io's surface is believed to be caused by the sulfur and salts brought to the surface by this volcanic activity—an activity identified nowhere else in the solar system but on Earth. Voyager 2 took one last edge-on look at Jupiter's newly discovered ring, then followed Voyager 1 into deeper space and their rendezvous with Saturn.

Voyager 1 reached Saturn in November 1980 and focused its television camera on the planet's rings first observed by Galileo three hundred and seventy years ago. Galileo's primitive telescope had been able to define the rings only as two blobs of light on either side of the planet. Dutch Astronomer Christian Huygens realized the blobs were actually a ring girdling the planet. Pioneer 11's less sophisticated cameras, which had first viewed Saturn's rings in 1979, had been unable to provide enough definition and resolution to permit a count of Saturn's rings beyond what appeared to be six uniform bands. But as Voyager 1's cameras tracked across the rings and the spacecraft beamed its binary impulses nearly a billion miles back across to an Earth tracking station in Spain and from there by satellite to a T.V. monitor in Caltech's Jet Propulsion Laboratory, scientists were awed to discover that what had been previously thought of as six bands was now over a thousand separate rings including one seemingly braided ring 50,000 miles above the planet's cloud-covered surface. Staring at this newly discovered braided ring on his T.V. monitor, astronomer Bradford Smith said, "It boggles the mind that it even exists!"

Voyager's photographs of Saturn boggled the minds of more than astronomers. No matter how awed one had been by the photographs sent back from Jupiter, Saturn seemed to have ever more wondrous sights and mysteries. Its banded atmosphere revealed itself to contain storms like Jupiter's—and yet unlike Jupiter's. The unexpected glory of its rings seemed to defy the laws of astronomy: there were braided rings, lopsided rings, rings that had rings and ringlets fanning out from the planet's surface like the grooves of a longplaying record; and dark spokes inexplicably radiating from the planet through its brightest ring.

Voyager discovered three new moons of Saturn and photographed four of its small moons, Dione, Tethys, Rhea and Mimas—all with diameters ranging from 200 to 1,000 miles and all seeming to have rock cores encased in a thin layer of ice. Mimas, nicknamed the Death Star by the Voyager team because of its resemblance to Darth Vadar's battleship in the science-fiction movie *Star Wars*, is dominated by a gigantic meteor crater nearly one-fourth that moon's diameter. Had the meteor been any larger, it would probably have shattered Mimas to pieces. Dione, too, is heavily cratered with a deep valley that fractures its crust like an eggshell halfway across its poles. Titan, the most intriguing moon in the solar system because it has an atmosphere, turned out to be unfit for any terrestrial form of life. Although its nitrogen rich atmosphere was surprisingly similar to our own, Titan, the largest of Saturn's moons and twice the size of ours, is covered by seas of liquid nitrogen and freezing hydrocarbons. Said Stanford radio astronomer Von Eshleman, "Titan could be considered a terrestrial planet in deep freeze."

Voyager discovered three new moons of Saturn and photographed four of its small moons, Dione, Tethys, Rhea and Mimas—all with diameters ranging from 200 to 1,000 miles and all seeming to have rock cores encased in a thin layer of ice. Mimas, nicknamed the Death Star by the Voyager team because of its resemblance to Darth Vadar's battleship in the science-fiction movie *Star Wars*, is dominated by a gigantic meteor crater nearly one-fourth that moon's diameter. Had the meteor been any larger, it would probably have shattered Mimas to pieces. Dione, too, is heavily cratered with a deep valley that fractures its crust like an eggshell halfway across its poles. Titan, the most intriguing moon in the solar system because it has an atmosphere, turned out to be unfit for any terrestrial form of life. Although its nitrogen rich atmosphere was surprisingly similar to our own, Titan, the largest of Saturn's moons and twice the size of ours, is covered by seas of liquid nitrogen and freezing hydrocarbons. Said Stanford radio astronomer Von Eshleman, "Titan could be considered a terrestrial planet in deep freeze."

Voyager 2 passed within 745 miles of the Saturnian rings and sent back 15,000 photographs over one billion miles to scientists. The Voyager 1 estimate that Saturn had over a thousand rings was changed to thousands of rings. Thought generally to be a mile deep, the rings were found to be only 500 feet thick in spots, containing billions of tiny ice-rock particles which create a disclike halo over 620,000

miles wide around the planet. Paradoxically, the Voyager 2's closer inspection of Saturn's rings raised more questions than it answered.

It is dismaying to think that although Voyager 2 now continues out into ever deeper space toward its meetings with Uranus in 1986 and Neptune in 1989, by the time our less than one-ton emissary from Earth reaches those planets, budget cuts might eliminate any person or installation here able to listen and evaluate its transmissions.

The National Aeronautical and Space Administration's planetary exploration program—the program which, during the past fifteen years, has provided us with our first close-up looks at cratered, sun-baked Mercury and a continent-sized landmass beneath Venus' sulphuric clouds, which has given us a pink sunset over a brick-red desertscape on Mars and has revealed to us the extraordinarily complex and beautiful wave patterns at the edge of Jupiter's stormy Great Red Spot, which has photographed a nearly 200-mile high eruption of a volcano on Io a half-billion miles away, and given us the dazzling views of Saturn's rings—this astonishing scientific accomplishment which is America's own NASA planetary exploration program is now threatened with extinction.

NASA has already had to cancel its spacecraft share of its participation with Western Europe to send two unmanned spacecraft into high, looping orbits over the as yet unexplored poles of our own Sun.

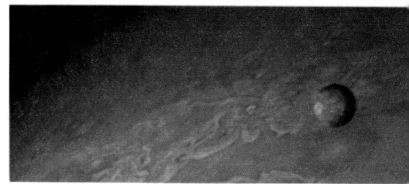

Io orbiting Jupiter in the vicinity of its turbulent southern hemisphere.

A model of the highly successful Voyager 1 spacecraft whose photographs, sent back during its Jupiter flyby in March, 1979, thrilled the world.

Missed also has been the opportunity to intercept Halley's Comet in 1986, which comes within range of a launch only every seventy-six years. There is even a chance that Project Galileo, an enterprise that is to place an unmanned spacecraft in orbit around Jupiter and release a probe directly into that planet's mysterious atmosphere, will be dismantled as well.

The passion to explore is at the heart of mankind. It is difficult for the visitor to the National Air and Space Museum to believe that because of an obsession with the problems of the present, we will deny ourselves the blazing potential that future space explorations promise. Just as Magellan, Columbus and all those others sailed our planet's uncharted seas, so should we continue to send our starships into space. How can we want to stop exploration of unknown worlds now any more than we would have wanted to cease exploration of our own then? America as we know it would not even exist without those early explorers. The future of any age will not be denied. For every visitor knows, when he comes to the Museum to share in one of mankind's oldest dreams, when he looks upon all the wonders displayed in NASM's galleries, that he is looking upon the footprints of humanity on its long, arduous, occasionally halting, but altogether satisfying, admirable and inevitable journey to the stars.

Sunset on Mars, courtesy of Viking 1.

Spacearium

After the exhausting excitement of seeing the Museum's gallery exhibits, simply resting in a comfortable armchair in the quiet, darkened 250-seat Albert Einstein Spacearium while tranquil music washes over one through the superb sound system would seem enough of a treat. But just as the theater's presentation captivated Museum visitors by taking them on a flying tour of the Earth, the Spacearium show's striking introduction to the stars intrigues visitors by taking them on a fascinating and informative journey to worlds beyond our blue planet.

"New Eyes on the Universe," the show in NASM's Albert Einstein Spacearium, is a half-hour voyage into outer space with visual effects by one of the world's finest planetarium instruments, a Carl Zeiss Model VI (given the National Air and Space Museum by the West German government as a Bicentennial gift), and over 200 modified projectors hidden behind the planetarium's 70-foot-diameter dome, which is made of aluminum sheet with millions of tiny, evenly spaced perforations.

The show tells the story of space-age astronomy. In the last quarter century, scientists have begun to use amazing new tools to study the heavens. No longer tied solely to ground-based observatories, today's scientists probe into the far reaches of space with electronic eyes orbiting high above the atmosphere.

Aerospace Chronology

December, 1919: Smithsonian Institution publishes Robert H. Goddard's classic paper. *A Method of Reaching Extreme Altitudes.*

March 16, 1926: Robert Goddard demonstrates successful operation of a liquid-fuel rocket at Auburn, Massachusetts. His rocket attains a distance of 184 feet in 2½ seconds, the "Kitty Hawk" of rocketry.

October 3, 1942: First successful flight of the German A-4 (V-2) liquid-fuel rocket-propelled ballistic missile, from Peenemunde, Germany.

October 14, 1947: Capt. Charles E. Yeager becomes the first pilot to exceed the speed of sound, flying the air-launched experimental Bell XS-1 rocket-propelled research airplane to Mach 1.06, 700 mph (1,127 kph) at 43,000 feet (13,106.40 meters), over Muroc Dry Lake, California.

August 25, 1949: First emergency use of a partial-pressure pilot-protection suit, by Maj. Frank K. Everest, on board the Bell X-1, following loss of cabin pressurization at 69,000 feet (21,031 meters.)

December, 1951: Richard Whitcomb verifies the Area Rule concept to reduce aircraft drag characteristics at transonic and supersonic speeds. This concept, popularized as the so-called "Coke bottle" or "wasp waist" shape, is first verified by flight testing on the Convair F-102.

November 20, 1953: Research test pilot A. Scott Crossfield becomes the first pilot to exceed Mach 2, twice the speed of sound, in an experimental air-launched rocket-propelled Douglas D-558-2 sky-rocket. The plane attains Mach 2.005, approximately 1,328 mph (2,138 kph) over Edwards Air Force Base, California.

September 27, 1956: Capt. Milburn Apt, United States Air Force, becomes the first pilot to fly three times faster than the speed of sound, reaching Mach 3.196, 2,094 mph (3,371 kph) in the Bell X-2. Apt is killed, however, when the plane tumbles out of control into the Mojave Desert.

October 4, 1957: Sputnik 1, the first man-made earth satellite, is placed in orbit by the Soviet Union—the dawn of the Space Age.

November 3, 1957: Launch of Sputnik 2, carrying dog, Laika, first living creature to orbit the Earth.

January 31, 1958: Explorer 1, the first United States satellite, is successfully launched.

September 12, 1959: Soviet Union launches Luna 2, the first man-made object to impact the Moon.

September 17, 1959: First powered flight of the North American X-15 hypersonic research airplane, by test pilot A. Scott Crossfield, at Edwards Air Force Base, California.

October 4, 1959: Soviet Union launches Luna 3, the first spacecraft to photograph the lunar farside.

April 1, 1960: Tiros I, the first weather satellite, is launched by the United States.

August 16, 1960: Capt. Joseph W. Kittinger, Jr., makes a record parachute descent by jumping from the balloon *Excelsior III* at an altitude of 102,800 feet and free-falling 17 miles before opening his parachute at 17,500 feet.

1961: The North American X-15 research airplane completes the first manned flights of a winged aircraft to Mach 4, 5, and 6.

April 12, 1961: Maj. Yuri Gagarin completes the first manned space flight by making a one-orbital mission aboard the Soviet spacecraft *Vostok*.

May 5, 1961: Alan B. Shepard, Jr., becomes the first American astronaut to enter space, making a 15-minute suborbital flight.

September 12, 1961: The Hawker P.1127 experimental vectored-thrust research airplane completes its first transition from vertical takeoff to horizontal flight, and back to a vertical landing. The P.1127 serves as the basis for the world's first operational VTOL fighter, the Hawker-Siddeley Harrier.

February 20, 1962: United States astronaut Lt. Col. John Glenn becomes the first American to orbit the Earth, aboard the Mercury spacecraft *Friendship 7*.

July 10, 1962: The United States launches Telstar I, providing the first transatlantic satellite television relay.

August 27, 1962: Mariner 2, the first spacecraft to conduct a fly-by of another planet (Venus), is launched by the United States.

June 16, 1963: Valentina Tereshkova becomes the first woman in space, aboard the Russian Vostok 6.

March 18, 1965: Alexei Leonov becomes the first person to perform an extra-vehicular activity (EVA, or spacewalk), during the Voskhod 2 mission.

June 3, 1965: Edward H. White II becomes the first American to perform an extravehicular activity, during the flight of Gemini 4.

November 16, 1965: Soviet Venus 3 spacecraft is launched, and on March 1, 1966, becomes the first man-made object to impact Venus.

January 31, 1966: The Soviet Union launches Luna 9, the first unmanned spacecraft to make a soft landing on the Moon.

June 1, 1966: The first American spacecraft to make a soft landing on the Moon, Surveyor 1, is launched.

July 12, 1966: First test flight of the Northrop/NASA M2-F2 lifting-body testbed by Milton O. Thompson, at Edwards Air Force Base, California. The lifting-body concept was being studied as one means of accomplishing manned re-entry from space.

August 10, 1966: The United States launches Lunar Orbiter 1, which provides high-resolution photographs for the selection of Apollo landing sites.

October 3, 1967: Maj. William J. Knight sets a new unofficial world airspeed record for winged aircraft of 4,534 mph (Mach 6.72) in the North American X-15A-2; this is the fastest winged flight and the fastest X-15 flight ever made.

December 21—27, 1968: Apollo 8, piloted by astronauts Frank Borman, James Lovell, Jr., and William Anders, becomes the first manned spacecraft to orbit the Moon.

May 18-26, 1969: Astronauts Thomas Stafford, Eugene Cernan, and John Young test the Lunar Module in lunor orbit in Apollo 10 mission.

July 20, 1969: Apollo 11 astronauts Neil Armstrong and Edwin Aldrin become the first humans to step on another celestial body when they land on the Moon.

November 24, 1970: First test flight of the NASA supercritical wing, developed by Richard T. Whitcomb, on a North American—Rockwell T-2C trainer.

May 30, 1971: The United States launches Mariner 9, the first spacecraft to survey the planet Mars from orbit.

March 3, 1972: Pioneer 10, the first spacecraft to visit the outer planets, is launched from Cape Kennedy.

December 7—9, 1972: Flight of Apollo 17; astronauts Eugene Cernan, Harrison Schmidt, and Ronald Evans are the last Apollo crew to visit the Moon.

May 25—June 22, 1973: Astronauts Charles Conrad, Paul Weitz, and Joseph Kerwin undertake Skylab 2 mission, launching from Cape Kennedy for a rendezvous with the Skylab Orbital Workshop launched (as Skylab 1) on May 14. They make extensive repairs to the damaged workshop before beginning a program of planned experiments.

November 3, 1973: Mariner 10, the first spacecraft to fly-by Mercury, is launched by the United States.

July 15—24, 1975: Apollo-Soyuz Test Project astronauts Alexei Leonov, Valeriy Kubasov, Thomas Stafford, Donald Slayton, and Vance Brand take part in the first international manned space mission.

September 9, 1975: Viking II is launched toward Mars.

August 20, 1975: The United States launches Viking I, its first Mars lander, which soft-lands July 20, 1976.

August 20, 1977: Voyager 2 is launched by the United States to fly-by Jupiter, Saturn and beyond.

September 5, 1977: Voyager I is launched. Its trajectory will take it to the vicinity of Jupiter sooner than Voyager 2.

September 29, 1977: Salyut 6 space laboratory is launched by the Soviet Union. The spacecraft has been re-supplied and occupied by cosmonauts for as long as 139 days.

April 12, 1981: First flight of Space Shuttle *Columbia*, the world's first reusable manned-space vehicle, by astronauts John W. Young and Robert L. Crippen.

Technical Appendix

The technical data presented here apply to the major spacecraft appearing in this book. The numbers at the left of each entry refer to the pages on which the vehicle is illustrated.

Milestones of Flight

14–15 BELL X-1—*GLAMOROUS GLENNIS*

Wingspan	8.54m (28 ft.)
Length	9.41m (30.90 ft.)
Height	3.31m (10.85 ft.)
Weight	Launch configuration, 5.557kg (12,250 lb.) Landing configuration, 3,175kg (7,000 lb.)
Engine	Reaction Motors, Inc. XLR-11-RM-3 (Model A6000C4), 6,000-lb. static thrust

16–17 NORTH AMERICAN X-15

Wingspan	6.82m (22.36 ft.)
Length	15.47m (50.75 ft.)
Height	396m (13 ft.)
Weight	Launch configuration, 17,237kg (38,000 lb.) Landing configuration, 5,670kg (12,500 lb.)
Engine	Thiokol (Reaction Motors) XLR-99-RM-2, 57,000-lb. thrust at sea level

18–19 GEMINI 4

Length	5.6m (18 ft. 4 in.) in orbit; 2.3m (7 ft. 4 in.) at splashdown
Base diameter	Adapter, 3.1m (10 ft.); spacecraft, 2.3m (7 ft. 6 in)
Launch vehicle	Titan II

21 FRIENDSHIP 7

Length	3.4m (11 ft.) in orbit; 2.2m (7 ft. 3 in.) at splashdown
Base diameter	1.9m (6 ft. 2½ in.)
Weight	1,344kg (2,987 lb.) in orbit; 1,100kg (2,422 lb.) at splashdown
Launch vehicle	Atlas

25 GODDARD'S MARCH 16, 1926, ROCKET

Length	6.7m (22 ft.)
Diameter	46cm (18 in.)
Weight (empty)	86kg (190 lb.)
Fuel	Gasoline, 55kg (112 lb.)
Oxidizer	Liquid oxygen, 64 kg (140 lb.)
Thrust	446kg (985 lb.)

25 THE 1941 GODDARD ROCKET

Length	6.7m (22 ft.)
Diameter	46cm (18 in.)
Weight (empty)	86 kg (190 lb.)
Weight of propellants	Gasoline, 55kg (112 lb.) Liquid oxygen, 64kg (140 lb.)
Thrust (static test)	446kg (985 lb.)

31 APOLLO 11 COMMAND MODULE *COLUMBIA*

Length	3.2m (10 ft. 7 in.)
Weight	5,896kg (13,000 lb.)
Base diameter	3.9m (12.8 ft)
Launch vehicle	Saturn V

Rocketry and Space Flight

42 GODDARRD'S "HOOPSKIRT" ROCKET (1928)

Height	4.5m (14 ft. 8 in.)
Weight	12.93kg (28.5 lb)
Fuel	Gasoline
Oxidizer	Liquid oxygen

42 GODDARD'S MAY 4, 1926, ROCKET

Length	1.95m (6 ft. 4 in.)
Weight	2.5kg (5.5 lb.)
Fuel	Gasoline
Oxidizer	Liquid oxygen

Satellites

64 BIOSATELLITE 2

Diameter	102cm (40 in.)
Length	122cm (48 in.)
Weight (launch)	236kg (515 lb.)
Apogee	236km (203 mi.)
Period	90.8 min.
Launch vehicle	Delta
Launch date	Sept. 7, 1967

Apollo to the Moon

68 *FREEDOM* 7 MERCURY SPACECRAFT

Diameter	2m (6 ft. 6 in.) max.
Length	2.8m (9 ft. 2 in.) at launch
Weight	1,660kg (3,650 lb.) at launch; 1,100kg (2,422 lb.) as exhibited
Launch vehicle	Redstone

71, 72 GEMINI 7 SPACECRAFT

Length	5.6m (18 ft. 4 in.) in orbit; 2.3m (7 ft. 4 in.) at splashdown
Base diameter	Adapter, 3.1m (10 ft.); Spacecraft, 2.3m (7 ft. 6 in.)
Launch vehicle	Titan II

73 GEMINI 9 SPACECRAFT and AUGMENTED TARGET DOCKING ADAPTER (ATDA)
Gemini: See Gemini 7 above

ATDA:

Length	3.3m (10 ft. 11 in.) without nose shroud
Diameter	1.52m (5 ft)
Weight	772kg (1,700 lb.)
Launch vehicle	Atlas

78–79 F-1 ENGINES

Function	Cluster of five providing 3.4 million kg (7.5 million lb.) of thrust for Saturn V first stage
Thrust	690,000kg (1,522,000 lb.)
Propellants	Kerosene (fuel) and liquid oxygen (oxidizer)
Length	5.8 (19 ft.) with nozzle extension
Diameter	3.8m (12 ft. 4 in.) with nozzle extension

82 APOLLO 10's LUNAR MODULE, *SNOOPY*
Ascent stage only:

Height	3.8m (12 ft. 4 in.)
Width	4.3m (14 ft. 1 in.)
Weight	4.635kg (10.300 lb.)

86–87 Interior of APOLLO 17 LUNAR LANDER

Habitable volume	4.48 cu m (160 cu. ft.)
Pressurized volume	6.58 cu m (235 cu. ft.)
Cabin temperature	24°C. (75°F.)

88–89 APOLLO LUNAR MODULE

Height	7m (22 ft. 11 in.), legs extended
Diameter	9.4m (31 ft.) diagonally across landing gear
Weight Earth launch	14,700kg (32,400 lb.)
LM (dry)	3,900kg (8,600 lb.)
Volume Pressurized	6.7 cu m (235 cu. ft.)
Habitable	4.5 cu. m (160 cu. ft.)

Space Hall

110, 118–119, 120–121 SKYLAB ORBITAL WORKSHOP

Length	14.66m (48 ft.)
Diameter	6.58m (21.6 ft.)
Weight	35.380kg (78,622 lb.)
Launch vehicle	Saturn V

114–115, 116–117 SKYLAB'S MULTIPLE DOCKING ADAPTER AND AIRLOCK MODULE

Length	10.67m (35 ft.)
Diameter	3.05m (10 ft.)
Weight	28.485kg (63,300 lb.)

123, 124 SKYLAB 4 APOLLO COMMAND MODULE

Diameter	3.9m (12 ft. 10 in.) max.
Length	3.2m (10 ft. 7 in.)
Weight	5,896kg (13,000 lb.)
Launch vehicle	Saturn 1B

130–133 APOLLO-SOYUZ TEST PROJECT (ASTP)

Apollo

Command module

Base diameter	3.90m (12.8 ft.)
Length	3.66m (12 ft.)
Weight	5.896kg (13,000 lb.)

Service module

Diameter	3.9m (12.8 ft.)
Length	6.71 m (22 ft.)
Weight at launch	24.947kg (55,000 lb.)

Docking module

Diameter	1.52m (5 ft.)
Length	3.05m (10 ft.)
Weight	1.882kg (4,155 lb.)
Launch Vehicle	Saturn IB

Soyuz

Orbital Module

Diameter	2.29m (7.5 ft.)
Length	2.65m (8.7 ft.)
Weight	1.224kg (2.700 lb.)

Descent module

Diameter	2.29m (7.5 ft.)
Length	2.20m (7.2 ft.)
Weight	2,802kg (6,200 lb.)

Instrument module

Diameter	2.77m (9.75 ft.)
Length	2.29m (7.5 ft.)
Weight	2,654kg (5,850 lb.)

The Space Shuttle

136–137 M2-F3 "LIFTING BODY"

Length	6.8m (22 ft. 2 in.)
Span	2.9m (9 ft. 7 in.)
Height	2.5m (8 ft. 10 in.)
Weight	2,720kg (6,000 lb.) empty; 4,540kg (10,000 lb.) fueled
Speed	1,718km per hr (1,066 m per hr) max. achieved
Altitude	21,800m (71,500 ft.) max. achieved
Mach number	1.5 max. achieved

135, 139–141 SPACE SHUTTLE

Length	Complete assembly, 56.1m (184 ft.) Orbiter, 37.3m (122.3 ft.)
Orbiter wingspan	32.8m (78 ft.)
Launch weight	Complete assembly, 1.89 million kg (4.4 million lb.)
Thrust at launch	3 million kg (6.7 million lb.

Exploring the Planets

154–155 VOYAGER

Diameter of reflector	3.66m (12 ft.)
Launch weight	825kg (1,820 lb.)
Length of magnetometer boom	13m (43 ft.)
Launch vehicle	Titan 3E Centaur
Launch dates	Voyager 2, Aug. 20, 1977; Voyager 1, Sept. 5, 1977

144–145 SPACE TELESCOPE

Weight	11,000kg (24,000 lb.)
Length	13.1m (43 ft.)
Diameter	4.26m (14 ft.)
Optical	2.4m (94 in.)
Telescope Assembly	reflecting cassegrain-type telescope
Launch Vehicle	Space Shuttle

Bibliography

Allen, Everett S., *A Wind to Shake the World: The Story of the 1938 Hurricane.* Boston, 1976.

Armstrong, Neil, et al., *First on the Moon: The Astronauts' Own Story.* Boston, 1970.

Asimov, Isaac, *Of Time, Space, and Other Things.* New York, 1975.

Belew, Leland F., *Skylab, Our First Space Station.* Washington, D.C., 1977.

Carpenter, M. Scott, et al., *We Seven, by the Astronauts Themselves.* New York, 1962.

Cartwright, Edgar M., ed., *Apollo Expeditions to the Moon.* Washington, D.C., 1975.

Clarke, Arthur C., *The Coming of the Space Age.* New York, 1967.

———, *The Promise of Space.* New York, 1968.

———, *The View from Serendip.* New York, 1977.

———, and the eds. of "Life," *Man and Space* (Life Science Library). New York, 1969.

Collins, Michael, *Carrying the Fire: An Astronaut's Journey.* New York, 1974.

Cooke, H. L., and James Dean, *Eyewitness to Space.* New York, 1973.

Cooper, Henry S. F., Jr., *A House In Space.* New York, 1976.

———, *Thirteen: The Flight That Failed.* New York, 1972.

Cunningham, Walter, *The All-American Boys.* New York, 1977.

Dornberger, Walter, *V-2.* New York, 1979.

Durant, Frederick C., III, "Robert Goddard and the Smithsonian Institution," in *First Steps Toward Space.* Washington, D.C., 1974.

———, "Robert H. Goddard: Accomplishments of the Roswell Years (1930–1945)." (to be published).

Engle, Eloise, and Arnold S. Lott, *Man in Flight: Biomedical Achievements in Aerospace.* Annapolis, Md., 1979.

Ezell, Edward C., and Linda Ezell. *The Partnership: A History of the Apollo-Soyuz Test Project.* Washington, D.C., 1978.

Froehlich, Walter, *Apollo Soyuz.* Washington, D.C., 1976.

Gatland, Kenneth, *Frontiers of Space.* New York, 1969.

———, *Manned Spacecraft.* New York, 1976.

———, *Missiles and Rockets.* New York, 1975.

———, *Robot Explorers.* New York, 1972.

Grissom, Virgil "Gus," *Gemini!* New York, 1968.

Hacker, Barton C., and James Grimewood, *On the Shoulders of Titans: A History of Project Gemini.* Washington, D.C., 1977.

Hallion, Richard P., *American Flight Research and Flight Testing: An Overview from the Wright Brothers to the Space Shuttle.* Society of Experimental Test Pilots. vol. 13, No. 3.

———, *Supersonic Flight: The Story of the Bell X-1 and Douglas D-558.* New York, 1972.

———, and Tom D. Crouch, eds., *Apollo: Ten Years Since Tranquillity Base.* Washington, D.C., 1979.

Harris, Michael, "The Junk in Outer Space." *The Progressive.* Nov., 1978.

Johnson, Richard D., ed., *Space Settlements: A Design Study.* Washington, D.C., 1977.

Lewis, Richard S., *Appointment on the Moon.* New York, 1969.

Ley, Willy, *Rockets, Missiles and Men in Space.* New York, 1968.

Mohler, Stanley R., and Bobby H. Johnson, *Wiley Post, His Winnie Mae, and the World's First Pressure Suit.* Washington, D.C., 1971.

Murphy, Lynne C., *Rockets, Missiles, and Spacecraft of the National Air and Space Museum, Smithsonian Institution.* Washington, D.C., 1976.

O'Neill, Gerald K., *The High Frontier.* New York, 1978.

Stine, G. Harry, *Third Industrial Revolution,* New York, 1979.

Swenson, Lloyd, Jr., James M. Grimewood, and Charles C. Alexander, *This New Ocean: A History of Project Mercury.* Washington, D.C., 1966.

Von Braun, Wernher, and Frederic Ordway, *A History of Rocketry and Space Travel.* New York, 1975.

———, Silvio A. Bedini, and Fred L. Whipple, *Moon, Man's Greatest Adventure.* New York, 1973.

Wells, Whiteley and Karegeannes *Origins of NASA Names.* NASA SP-4402, Nasa History Series

Wilding-White, T.M., *Jane's Pocket Book of Space Exploration.* New York, 1977.

Young, John and Robert Crippen, "Our Phenomenal First Flight," *The National Geographic,* vol. 160, No. 4, October 1981.

Index

Numbers in roman type refer to text pages. Numbers in *italic* type refer to pages on which illustrations appear. *n* refers to a note.

A Note on the Photography

If the exhibits as they appear in this book seem as real and lively to the readers as the experience of visiting the Museum, then the three photographers and myself have achieved our objective. The photographers never had previously the opportunity, or the challenge, of attempting to represent such a vast, diverse museum experience through the camera, from scratch. The effort proved an extraordinary experience in itself.

It was necessary, for instance, for one of the photographers to spend a week photographing the huge murals that dominate the main entrance to the Museum. To do this he had to perch in a cage 50 feet above the ground, holding his breath and taking pictures with a 45-second exposure, patiently guessing that he would miss the tremor caused by the new Metro under the Museum—a tremor which could be felt only on his high, extended platform.... Photographing the insides of the Apollo Command Module brought home the recognition that it had not been designed for photography. But the acute discomforts to the photographer of maneuvering in that restricted space to get his shots demonstrated, as nothing else could, the truly astonishing feat of the three men who lived in that Module for a full week.

During the actual shooting of the many exhibits we were mindful of the fact that in a true peoples' museum we had to conduct our work without hindering the enjoyment of the visitors. We hope we succeeded in this. It was interesting to note how many people were themselves enjoying the fun of photography. And we noticed, with amusement, that whenever we were attempting to photograph the public itself, people would observe our attempts and curtail their own examination of the exhibit, politely stepping aside, not realizing that their fascination with the riches the Museum has to offer was exactly what we were after. Nevertheless, our thanks to those adults and children who do appear in this book, for making that part of our task such a pleasure. Our thanks, too, to all the Museum staff who so ably assisted us. But the photographers especially would like to thank E.J. Thomas, who helped us to get into position for many particularly difficult shots, and who was an unfailing mainstay throughout the months of our work in the Museum.

David Larkin
London